T0063798

WALKING
WASHINGTON, D.C.

WALKING
WASHINGTON, D.C.

THE BEST OF THE CITY
Barbara Noe Kennedy

Photography by Lisa A. Walker

NATIONAL GEOGRAPHIC

Washington, D.C.

WALKING
WASHINGTON, D.C.

CONTENTS

6 INTRODUCTION
8 VISITING WASHINGTON, D.C.
10 USING THIS GUIDE

PART 1

PAGE 12
WHIRLWIND TOURS

14 D.C. IN A DAY
18 D.C. IN TWO DAYS
26 D.C. FOR FUN
30 D.C. WITH KIDS
34 AFRICAN-AMERICAN HERITAGE
38 EMBASSY ROW

PART 2

PAGE 42
WASHINGTON'S NEIGHBORHOODS

46 NATIONAL MALL
68 CAPITOL HILL
86 DOWNTOWN
106 WHITE HOUSE & AROUND
126 DUPONT CIRCLE & BEYOND
142 GEORGETOWN
158 OLD TOWN ALEXANDRIA

Previous pages:
Jefferson Memorial;
opposite: tourists on
bicycles in front of
SunTrust building;
right: bust of George
Washington, National
Portrait Gallery;
top right: view from
POV bar; bottom
right: World War II
Memorial

PART 3

PAGE 176
TRAVEL ESSENTIALS

178 TRAVEL ESSENTIALS
181 HOTELS

188 INDEX
191 CREDITS

Introduction

Everyone owns the National Mall, but no one ever offers to mow it. That's Washington, D.C., a city built on compromise and still bristling under the arrangement. When the capital district was sited here in 1790, this partial swamp was intended to bring a southerly sensibility to the nation's northern economic center. It's hard to say if that worked. John F. Kennedy quipped: "Washington is a city of southern efficiency and northern charm." D.C. is a city of such symbolic magnitude and structural presence that the people who live here, and the qualities that make us unique, are often obscured. The oddest thing to say about the nation's capital is that it's "a city of transients." What city worth its salt isn't? Any other city with this sort of turnover would be celebrated as a hotbed of reinvention. And that's exactly what Washington is today. A buzzing hub of interconnected neighborhoods (pedal a Capital Bikeshare cycle from Logan Circle to Shaw). A community of hungry explorers (feast up 14th Street N.W. or devour Union Market) with a spirit for invention (the gin rickey was first stirred in D.C.). A creative and globalized set of brainy bureaucrats and socialized millennials who love their local brew (Compass Coffee is tops, DC Brau is hops). But here's a concession we can all agree on: Washington is not an "either/or" city. It's a "both/and" kind of town. So get your walking shoes on and go explore the District of Columbia with an uncompromising sense of discovery.

The oddest thing to say about the nation's capital is that it's "a city of transients." What city worth its salt isn't?

George W. Stone
Editor in Chief, National Geographic Traveler *magazine*

Visiting Washington, D.C.

A noble capital glowing with marble monuments, Washington, D.C., offers public parks, more than 50 museums (many with free admission), and year-round cultural events. But gridlock can snarl travelers as well as politicians. Here are some tips.

Washington in a Nutshell

The Father of the Country, George Washington himself, selected an unlikely, undeveloped spot on the Potomac River to build the nation's capital—the result of a compromise between the northern and southern states. French architect Pierre-Charles L'Enfant designed the Capital City, giving it a European flair centered around a grand esplanade—the National Mall—lined by the most important government buildings. From here, distinct neighborhoods fan out into a quadrant of districts (see sidebar opposite), home today to some 706,000 residents.

Visiting the Sights

Many sights have security measures in place, including bag checks and metal detectors. Entry to museums may be long during peak seasons and holidays. Be sure to pack for the day wisely to assist in getting through the line quickly; also, note that some sights prohibit

Washington, D.C., Day by Day

Open every day (with some exceptions for major holidays) All Smithsonian museums, including National Zoo, National Gallery of Art, monuments, and most government buildings.

Monday Many sights are closed, including the Anderson House, Carlyle House Historic Park, Dumbarton House, Dumbarton Oaks, Eastern Market, Gadsby's Tavern Museum, Lee-Fendall House, Phillips Collection, Octagon House, Stabler-Leadbeater Apothecary Museum, and Tudor Place Historic House & Garden.

Tuesday Sights closed include Decatur House, Gadsby's Tavern Museum (*Nov.–March*), Lee-Fendall House, Octagon House, President Woodrow Wilson House, and Stabler-Leadbeater Apothecary Museum (*Nov.–March*).

Wednesday Decatur House and Octagon House are closed.

Thursday Decatur House is closed.

Sat.–Sun. Most museums in the Capital City are open weekends. However Decatur House and the U.S. Supreme Court are closed. Octagon House is open Sat. but closed Sun.

Waves of shadow and refracted light infuse this courtyard shared by the Smithsonian American Art Museum and the National Portrait Gallery.

certain items, such as water bottles, sharp objects, etc. The White House is especially strict. Check websites ahead of time for more specific information.

In many places, including Ford's Theatre, Washington Monument, and National Archives, you can skip long lines if you preorder timed passes online for a small fee.

Be aware that some sights can only be visited by guided tour, at specific times. The itineraries in this book aim to accommodate such restrictions, but keep them in mind as you plan your tour of the places you most want to explore. Also, many attractions offer insightful guided interpretive tours, lectures, IMAX movies, and other

IN **THE KNOW**

The city is laid out in four quadrants, with the Capitol building in the center. North Capitol, South Capitol, and East Capitol Streets radiate from here, separating the city into quadrants (the Mall runs west from the Capitol building). So, when seeking a sight, first check the quadrant address, which indicates where it lies— N.W., N.E., S.W., or S.E. Be advised that many addresses can be found in more than one quadrant (for instance, there is a 4000 M St. in N.E., S.E., S.W., and N.W.—four different D.C. locations).

intriguing programs throughout the day. Check websites or call ahead of time to make the most of your visit to the Capital City.

Using This Guide

Each tour—which might be only a walk, or might also take advantage of the city's public transportation—is plotted on a map and has been planned to take into account opening hours and the times of day when sights are less crowded. Many end near restaurants or lively nightspots for evening activities.

Whirlwind Tours

Whirlwind Tours are for people who have only a day or a weekend to spend in the city and want to ensure that they see the best of the best. Choose your tour based on your available time and interests: One Day, Two Days, For Fun, With Kids, African-American Heritage, and Embassy Row.

Tips For the One-Day and Two-Day Tours, a Tips spread following each itinerary map provides insider information on detours from the key sights, extra places to see, nearby restaurants, and ideas for adapting the tours to suit your interests.

Sight Descriptions
In the Whirlwind Tours, key sights spreads following the maps provide descriptions of all the sights and practical information for visitors.

Neighborhood Tours

The seven neighborhood tours each begin with an introduction, followed by an itinerary map highlighting the key sights that make up the tour plus detailed key sight descriptions. Each tour is followed by an "in-depth" spread showcasing one major sight along the route, a "distinctly D.C." spread providing background information on a quintessential element that relates to that neighborhood, and a "best of" spread that groups sights thematically.

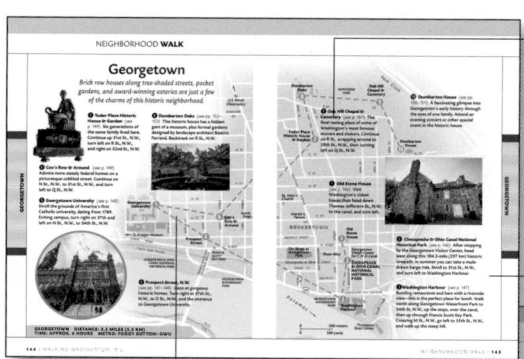

Itinerary Map A map of the neighborhood shows the locations of the key sights, Metro stations, and main streets.

Captions These captions briefly describe the key sights and give instructions on finding the next stop on the tour. Full descriptions of the sights may be found on the following pages.

Route Dotted lines link the key sights.

Price Ranges for Key Sites

$	$1–$5
$$	$6–$10
$$$	$11–$15
$$$$	$16–$20
$$$$$	$21+

Price Ranges for Good Eats
(for one person, excluding drinks)

$	Under $10
$$	$11–$20
$$$	$21–$35
$$$$	$36–$50
$$$$$	$51+

Key Sights Descriptions These spreads provide a detailed description and highlights for each sight, following the order on the map, plus each one's address, phone number, website, entrance fee, days closed, and nearest Metro station.

Good Eats Refer to these lists for a selection of locally recommended restaurants and cafés along the route.

Kayakers on the Potomac River, beneath
the Francis Scott Key Bridge

PART 1

Whirlwind Tours

D.C. in a Day

*Experience Washington's most popular sights
on this packed, one-day tour.*

⑤ Georgetown (see pp. 142–151)
Grab dinner at a stylish restaurant and, if you have extra time, poke into some of the city's poshest boutiques. Walk about a mile (1.6 km) to the Kennedy Center via paths alongside the Potomac—or take a cab.

⑥ Kennedy Center (see p. 17)
Finish your day with a dazzling show—ballet, symphony, opera, or theater—at this legendary cultural center.

**D.C. IN A DAY   DISTANCE: 7.5 MILES (12 KM)
TIME: 16 HOURS   METRO: SMITHSONIAN**

WHIRLWIND TOURS

4 Capitol Hill (see pp. 68–77) Swing past the U.S. Capitol, Library of Congress, and the U.S. Supreme Court then head to Union Station where you can hop on the Circulator bus (or take a cab) to Georgetown, about 5.5 miles (9 km) away.

3 National Air & Space Museum (see pp. 60–63) Applaud triumphs in air and space at the nation's most visited museum. Exiting onto Independence Ave., S.W., turn left; go up the hill to First St., S.E., and turn left.

Metro Center · E ST. · White House Visitor Center · PENNSYLVANIA AVENUE · Federal Triangle · 14TH ST. · 12TH ST. · 10TH ST. · 9TH ST. · 8TH ST. · 7TH ST. · 6TH ST. · 5TH ST. · Archives-Navy Memorial · D ST. · Judiciary Square · C ST. · CONSTITUTION AVE. · 395 · 4TH ST. · 3RD ST. · 2ND ST. · NEW JERSEY AVE. · FIRST ST. N.W. · LOUISIANA AVE. · CONSTITUTION AVE. · FIRST ST. N.E. · Union Station · Capitol Hill · U.S. Supreme Court

Museum of African American History and Culture · Nat. Museum of American History · Smithsonian · JEFFERSON DR. · Smithsonian · Nat. Mus. of Natural History · Smithsonian Castle · Freer Gallery of Art · Arts & Industries Building · **NATIONAL MALL** · Nat. Gallery Sculpture Garden · Hirshhorn Museum & Sculpture Garden · MADISON DRIVE · Nat. Gallery of Art West Building · Nat. Gallery of Art East Building · **National Air & Space Museum** · INDEPENDENCE AVE. · Capitol Reflecting Pool · **Northwest Southwest** · U.S. Capitol · **N.E. S.E.** · Library of Congress

1 Monuments & Memorials (see pp. 46–55) Celebrate democracy on an early morning stroll. Then head north a few blocks to the White House at 1600 Pennsylvania Ave., N.W.

2 White House (see pp. 118–121) See where P.O.T.U.S. lives, works, and entertains. Go south on 15th St., N.W., to the Mall and turn left on Jefferson Dr., S.W., to 7th St., S.W.

Tips

There's a lot to cover in Washington, D.C.—really too much for just one day!
That said, this tour jam-packs the biggest and the best the Capital City
has to offer, beginning at the National Mall and fanning out from there.

❶ Monuments & Memorials
(see pp. 46–55) The monuments and
memorials to the west of the National
Mall are open 24 hours a day; if you
arrive early, you're likely to have them
to yourself. The most stunning views
are from the steps of the Lincoln
Memorial looking east toward the sun-
rise, the Washington Monument, and
the U.S. Capitol. Beginning your day
at the ■ WASHINGTON MONUMENT,
a 2-mile (3 km) walk takes in the
■ NATIONAL WORLD WAR II
MEMORIAL, ■ VIETNAM VETERANS
MEMORIAL, ■ LINCOLN MEMORIAL,
■ MARTIN LUTHER KING, JR. MEMO-
RIAL, ■ FDR MEMORIAL, and ■ THOMAS
JEFFERSON MEMORIAL—all before the
rest of town has had a cup of coffee.

❷ White House (see pp. 118–121)
Even if you don't have tickets to tour
the President's House, there are other
experiences to be had. You can admire
the White House from all sides and
angles by following the exterior gate
all around, first along Pennsylvania
Avenue, then along the Ellipse
(see if you can pick out the sharp-
shooters on the roof). Or rest on a
park bench in ■ LAFAYETTE SQUARE,
just across Pennsylvania Avenue, and
gaze at the White House from afar.
You can also visit a lesser known presidential residence, the ■ OCTAGON
HOUSE (see p. 114), just a block away.
A good choice for brunch nearby is
the ■ HAMILTON (*600 14th St., N.W.,
tel 202-787-1000, thehamiltondc.com*),
a buzzing dining and entertainment
venue in the former Garfinckel's
department store. Come back in the
evening for a live concert.

**❸ National Air & Space
Museum** (see pp. 60–63) This
popular Smithsonian museum has
extended hours on certain dates (a
great time to go, when the crowds have
thinned)—check website for details.

❹ Capitol Hill (see pp. 68–77)
The major sights on "the Hill" line up along First Street, where the city's northeast and southeast quadrants align: the ■ **U.S. CAPITOL** (see pp. 78–81), the ■ **LIBRARY OF CONGRESS'S THOMAS JEFFERSON BUILDING** (see pp. 72–73), and the ■ **U.S. SUPREME COURT** (see pp. 74–75). If you want to tour the Capitol but haven't reserved tickets through your congressperson in advance, check if any of the first-come, first-served tickets are still available at the U.S. Capitol Visitor Center's lower level. Here you can also pop into ■ **EMANCIPATION HALL,** offering well-curated exhibits, original documents, videos, and an interesting cross section model of the Capitol dome.

❺ Georgetown (see pp. 142–151)
This fun neighborhood's main shopping streets are M Street, N.W., between 29th and 35th Streets, and Wisconsin Avenue, N.W., north of M Street. The ■ **CHESAPEAKE & OHIO CANAL** *(tel 301-739-4200, nps.gov/choh)* offers a scenic stroll along the historic waterway's towpath; the most charming section is between Thomas Jefferson Street and 31st Street, N.W. Or sit on a bench at ■ **GEORGETOWN WATERFRONT PARK** and enjoy

CUSTOMIZING **YOUR DAY**

The long National Mall, plus the miles of hallways awaiting inside each of the major museums, will test your walking stamina. Do your feet a favor by buying a ticket for a hop-on hop-off bus, which allows you to get on and off at popular stops. Big Bus Tours *(bigbustours.com)* and CitySights DC *(citysightsdc.com)* are among those offering this service.

watching D.C.'s movers and shakers at play with the Potomac as a backdrop. Stop at D.C. classic ■ **CLYDE'S OF GEORGETOWN** *(3236 M St., N.W., tel 202-333-9180)* to enjoy a pre-theater meal.

❻ Kennedy Center Take a free guided tour of this performing arts center, a "national living memorial" to the 35th president, or just wander beneath the flags of the ■ **HALL OF STATES** and ■ **HALL OF NATIONS,** plus the REACH—a 4.6-acre landscaped expansion (opened in September, 2019) with reflection pool, outdoor performance pavilions, and interactive art spaces. Better still, catch a show at one of the many theaters; the ■ **MILLENNIUM STAGE** *(kennedy-center.org)* has free shows at 6 p.m. most evenings. Need dinner? The Roof Terrace Restaurant *(tel 202-416-8555)* or the casual KC Café are options.

WHIRLWIND TOURS

D.C. in Two Days

Day One of a two-day tour takes in the National Mall followed by shopping in Georgetown and a show at the Kennedy Center

WHIRLWIND TOURS

To Key Bridge

Georgetown

M STREET

Chesapeake & Ohio Canal

PENNSYLVANIA AVE

FOGGY BOTTOM

Foggy Bottom-GWU

I ST. N.W.

H ST. N.W.

G ST.

23RD ST.

22ND ST.

21ST ST.

20TH ST.

⑦ Georgetown (see pp. 142–151) Shop and dine in one of the city's poshest neighborhoods. Then walk about a mile (1.6 km) to the Kennedy Center, via pathways alongside the Potomac—or take a cab.

⑥ Arlington National Cemetery (see p. 21) Pay homage to the soldiers who made the greatest sacrifice in conflicts as far back as the Civil War. When you're ready, walk about a mile (1.6 km) through Rosslyn and across Key Bridge to Georgetown, or take the Metro's blue line one stop to the Rosslyn station and walk across Key Bridge—or take a cab.

⑧
Kennedy Center
The Reach

⑧ Kennedy Center (see p. 17) Cap your day with a spectacular show at this venerable cultural center on the Potomac.

THEODORE ROOSEVELT MEMORIAL BRIDGE

CONSTITUTION

Vietnam Veterans Memorial

N.W.
S.W.

Lincoln Memorial

Reflecting Pool

Potomac

WEST POTOMAC PARK

Korean War Veterans Memorial

D.C. War Memorial

ARLINGTON MEMORIAL BRIDGE

INDEPENDENCE AVE

Martin Luther King, Jr. National Memorial

0   200 meters
0   200 yards

Arlington Cemetery

Arlington National Cemetery

⑥

OHIO DRIVE

D.C. IN TWO DAYS   DISTANCE: 7 MILES (11 KM)
TIME: APPROX. 16 HOURS   METRO: SMITHSONIAN

1 National Mall (see pp. 46–57) Take an early morning stroll around the National Mall's monuments, then head north to the White House, 1600 Pennsylvania Ave., N.W.

2 White House (see pp. 118–121) Explore the president's home (if you have reservations) or hit the nearby White House Visitor Center. Then go back to the Mall, and turn left on Madison Dr., N.W.

3 National Museum of American History (see pp. 58–59) Seek out Dorothy's ruby slippers and other cultural icons at this repository. Continue east along the Mall.

4 National Gallery of Art (see pp. 56–57) Take your pick: Byzantine altarpieces and French Impressionists in the West Building, or pop art and modern mobiles in the East Building. Or both. Then walk across to the other side of the Mall.

WHIRLWIND TOURS

5 National Air & Space Museum (see pp. 60–63) See the very vehicles that transported humankind from the aviation age into the space age. Then take the Metro's blue line from the Smithsonian station to the Arlington Cemetery station.

Tips

Two days give you a little more time to get to know this beautiful city. Spend Day One on the National Mall, with entertaining diversions to Georgetown and the Kennedy Center. Here are some tips to get you going, along with some possible alternatives to customize your visit.

WHIRLWIND TOURS

DAY 1

❷ White House (see pp. 118–121) Spend time at the ■ WHITE HOUSE VISITOR CENTER for fascinating insights into life at the White House past and present. If the nation's early history interests you, walk to the nearby ■ OCTAGON HOUSE (see p. 114), which served as the presidential residence for James Madison for a brief time after the British burned Washington in 1814. Another good option for history buffs is ■ DECATUR HOUSE on Lafayette Square (see pp. 111–112), home to the War of 1812 hero. Tour hours are limited, but beautifully curated special exhibitions in their parlor rooms offer another way to get a glimpse into early Washington. Check the website for what's on show.

❸ National Museum of American History (see pp. 58–59) The museum's docent-led highlights tours are an enjoyable way to make sure you hit the must-see sights in a short amount of time. And even if your packed schedule doesn't allow for a full visit to the fascinating ■ NATIONAL MUSEUM OF NATURAL HISTORY (see p. 56) next door, at the very least poke your head inside to admire the ■ AFRICAN BUSH ELEPHANT and the fabled ■ HOPE DIAMOND. For a breath of fresh air, the adjacent ■ BUTTERFLY HABITAT GARDEN (*gardens.si.edu*) draws butterflies to the urban setting. Immediately to the west, the ■ NATIONAL MUSEUM OF AFRICAN AMERICAN HISTORY AND CULTURE (see p. 36) tells the story of the United States from the African-American point of view. Across the National Mall, the iconic turreted ■ CASTLE (see sidebar p. 51) shows off a selection of fascinating objects from many of the Smithsonian's 19 area museums; enjoy a short film and a coffee, too.

❹ National Gallery of Art

(see pp. 56–57) Start at the front desk, where a "highlights" tour brochure pinpoints the most famous works in both buildings (they also have one for kids). If you are an art devotee, take one of the informative docent-led tours. Outside, the ■ **NATIONAL GALLERY OF ART SCULPTURE GARDEN** (*6th St. & Constitution Ave., N.W., tel 202-737-4215, nga.gov*) is an interesting stop for the whole family, with its larger-than-life installations (starring Claes Oldenburg and Joan Miró) and jazz concerts on summer Fridays; in winter its fountain transforms into a skating rink. If time allows, other fascinating museums on the Mall are the ■ **FREER GALLERY OF ART** and the ■ **ARTHUR M. SACKLER GALLERY** (*asia .si.edu*), both devoted to Asian art; the ■ **NATIONAL MUSEUM OF AFRICAN ART** (*africa.si.edu*); the curving ■ **NATIONAL**

National Museum of the American Indian

CUSTOMIZING **YOUR DAY**

The Smithsonian offers all kinds of fun goings-on, including festivals, films, talks, workshops, and shows—most for free. One of the most popular summer events is **Asia After Dark** at the Freer and Sackler Galleries, a night of tours, Bollywood-inspired dance classes, music, and specialty cocktails. **Cooking Up History** at the National Museum of American History dishes up the story behind favorite American foods with a guest chef in the on-site demonstration kitchen. Check *si.edu* for more offerings.

MUSEUM OF THE AMERICAN INDIAN (*nmai.si.edu*); and the ■ **HIRSHHORN MUSEUM AND SCULPTURE GARDEN** (*hirshhorn.si.edu*), showcasing contemporary art and culture. Remember, they're all free!

❻ Arlington National Cemetery

After absorbing the sobering rows of white headstones, take in the ceremonial ■ **CHANGING OF THE GUARD AT THE TOMB OF THE UNKNOWNS,** the moving ■ **ETERNAL FLAME** at John F. Kennedy's grave, and Robert E. Lee's graceful mansion, ■ **ARLINGTON HOUSE.** A pathway outside the cemetery entrance winds north to the nearby ■ **IWO JIMA MEMORIAL,** at the end of Memorial Bridge (*arlingtoncem etery.mil; Metro: Arlington Cemetery*).

WHIRLWIND TOURS

DAY
2

D.C. in Two Days

Explore Capitol Hill, a trendy new quarter, a classic restaurant beloved by political insiders, and a show at an award-winning regional theater on the second day of your two-day tour.

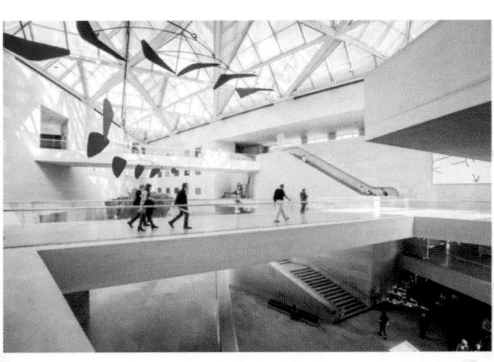

⑥ Old Ebbitt Grill

G ST.

15TH ST.

F ST.

Metro Center

E ST.

14TH ST. NW

PENNSYLVANIA

12TH ST.

9TH ST.

Federal Triangle

① 50

CONSTITUTION AVE.

NATIONAL

Smithsonian

JEFFERSON DR.

Smithsonian

14TH ST. SW

C ST.

D ST.

Tidal Basin

0   200 meters
0   200 yards

①

Fish Market

MAINE AVE. SW.

Washington Channel

⑤ Penn Quarter (see pp. 90–95) Find refreshment at one of this buzzing neighborhood's hip cafés near the Verizon Center, then visit your choice of several top-notch museums, such as the National Portrait Gallery. Go west on F St., N.W., to 15th St., N.W., and turn right to the corner of G St., N.W.

⑥ Old Ebbitt Grill (see p. 85)
Come dinnertime, keep an eye out for White House staffers as you dig into oysters at this legendary eatery. Take the Metro's red or green line from the Metro Center station to the Waterfront station and walk a block.

⑦ Arena Stage (see p. 25)
Round out your day with a show at this famous regional theater.

**D.C. IN TWO DAYS   DISTANCE: 3.25 MILES (5.2 KM)
TIME: APPROX. 15 HOURS   METRO: EASTERN MARKET**

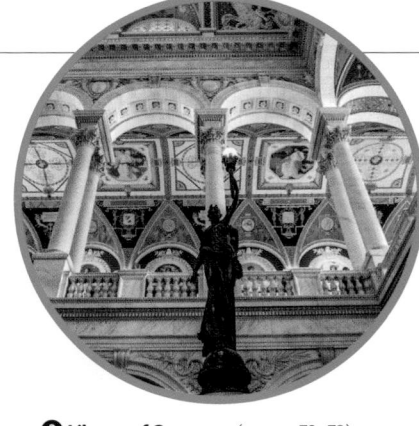

4 U.S. Supreme Court (see pp. 74–75) Pay homage to the highest court in the land. Go north one block to Constitution Ave., N.E., turn left, and walk to 7th St., N.W., turning right to reach the vicinity of F St., N.W.

3 Library of Congress (see pp. 72–73) Visit the dazzling neoclassical Thomas Jefferson Building, full of statues, columns, and frescoes—but where are the books? You'll find out. Go north, next door to 1st St., N.E.

Penn Quarter

Archives–Navy Memorial

Capitol Reflecting Pool

Northwest | Northeast
Southwest | Southeast

U.S. Capitol

U.S. Botanic Garden

U.S. Supreme Court

Library of Congress

CAPITOL HILL

Eastern Market

MALL

L'Enfant Plaza

Federal Center S.W.

Arena Stage

SOUTHWEST WATERFRONT

Waterfront

2 U.S. Capitol (see pp. 78–81) See the famous Rotunda and National Statuary Hall, and, if Congress is in session, watch politicians in action on the gallery floor. Then find the underground tunnel to the Library of Congress.

1 Eastern Market (see pp. 76–77) Take the blue line Metro from downtown and rub elbows with locals over blueberry buckwheat pancakes at Eastern Market. Then follow 7th St., S.E., north to E. Capitol St., N.E., and the Capitol.

Tips

Day Two of your two-day tour begins on Capitol Hill, where you can mix some local flavor with important national sites. Next explore the trendy Penn Quarter neighborhood with its happening restaurants and museums, dine at an iconic D.C. restaurant, and finish your day at an award-winning regional theater.

DAY 2

❶ Eastern Market (see pp. 76–77) In addition to those at the popular Eastern Market, breakfast options on the Hill include local favorites ■ **PETE'S DINER** at 212 2nd St., S.E. (*tel 202-544-7335*) and ■ **JIMMY T'S PLACE** at 501 E. Capitol St., S.E. (*tel 202-709-3557*).

❷ U.S. Capitol (see pp. 78–81) If there's no time for a tour, at least visit the U.S. Capitol Visitor Center's insightful, exhibit-filled ■ **EMANCIPATION HALL.** Get there early before the crowds begin, since you will have to stand in line for security. A stroll all around this giant classical edifice is enjoyable as well—go down the Capitol's south side along Independence Avenue to the lush greenhouses of the ■ **U.S. BOTANIC GARDEN** (see p. 156); then cross the front facade by the ■ **CAPITOL REFLECTING POOL** before climbing back up the Capitol's other side. You'll come across pocket gardens, hidden statues, and plenty of benches.

❸ Library of Congress (see pp. 72–73) The one-hour tour of this over-the-top beaux arts temple to books provides a great behind-the-scenes look at the library's history and design. Otherwise, pick up a self-guided tour brochure and find your way to the stunning ■ **GREAT HALL** and ■ **MAIN READING ROOM.**

❹ U.S. Supreme Court (see pp. 74–75) Want to see an oral argument at the nation's highest court, but don't want to spend the time standing in line? Hire a line stander! Seating for the first oral argument begins at 9:30 a.m.; to assure a seat, your line stander should be there at least 12 hours ahead of time. Search online for "DC line standing." The current rate is about $50 per hour.

❺ Penn Quarter (see pp. 90–95)
Grab a bite at one of the many trendy downtown restaurants, then spend the afternoon in one of the area's fabulous museums. Art lovers should head straight to the ■ SMITHSONIAN AMERICAN ART MUSEUM (see pp. 96–98) and the adjoining ■ NATIONAL PORTRAIT GALLERY (see pp. 98–99), displaying paintings, photographs, and sculptures of individuals who have come to define the United States as we know it, including portraits of every U.S. president. If you don't tarry, you'll have time for quick visits to at least two of the three. For food, ■ CLYDE'S OF GALLERY PLACE (707 7th St., N.W., tel 202-349-3700), ■ DISTRICT TACO (1309 F St., N.W., tel 202-347-7359), and ■ JALEO (480 7th St., N.W., tel 202-628-7949) are fun options.

❻ Old Ebbitt Grill (see p. 85)
Presidents Grant, Cleveland, Harding, and Theodore Roosevelt all hung out at this upscale, Victorian-style saloon, and today you still might spot a political insider or two. T. R. himself is said to have captured the walrus hanging at the bar. Seeking something a little more mod? The nearby ■ POV (see p. 84) rooftop bar at the hotel W Washington D.C. has cushioned sofas and great views. More restaurants are to the east, between 7th and 14th Sts., N.W.

CUSTOMIZING **YOUR DAY**

Prefer the great outdoors to indoor museums? Woodsy trails lace **Rock Creek Park** (tel 202-895-6000, nps.gov/rocr), once a favorite bird-watching destination for President Theodore Roosevelt. The **United States National Arboretum** (3501 New York Ave., N.E., tel 202-245-4523, usna.usda.gov) is a great place to stroll (though you'll need a car to get there). And **Theodore Roosevelt Island** (tel 703-289-2500, nps.gov/this), just north of Rosslyn, VA, is a hidden escape in the heart of the city.

❼ Arena Stage (arenastage.org).
Enjoy American plays at this renowned theater. An exciting redevelopment of the surrounding Wharf District, with its iconic ■ FISH MARKET, has graced the area with a bustling transit pier, marina, and boutique shops and restaurants.

The Library of Congress Main Reading Room

D.C. for Fun

D.C. isn't all about politics—enjoy a day in the places where Washingtonians frolic.

❶ Georgetown Shopping (see p. 28) Begin your day with a leisurely brunch followed by a dose of retail therapy at some of the city's trendiest shops. From M St., N.W., walk down to the Potomac River and turn left along the riverfront walkway.

❷ Lunch at Washington Harbour (see p. 28) Savor lunch on a shady outdoor terrace overlooking the Potomac River. Continue along the riverfront southeast to Thompson Boat Center.

❸ Kayak or Bike on the Potomac (see pp. 28–29) Enjoy some of D.C.'s prettiest scenery from the water or along a tree-shaded trail. Take the Metro's orange, blue, or silver line from the Foggy Bottom station to the Metro Center station and walk three blocks east on G St., N.W., then south two blocks on 15th St., N.W., to the W Washington D.C. hotel.

D.C. FOR FUN   DISTANCE: 2.5 MILES (4 KM)
TIME: APPROX. 13 HOURS   METRO: FOGGY BOTTOM

⑦ Nightcap at the Hamilton
(see p. 29) **End your fun day
with a nightcap at the Hamilton's
tucked-away piano bar.**

⑥ The Capitol Steps (see p. 29)
Enjoy some hilarious political satire
then walk north two blocks along
14th St., N.W.

**⑤ Drinks & Dinner on
14th Street** (see pp. 132–
133) Kick up your heels on
one of D.C.'s hippest streets.
From the U St.–African-
American Civil War
Memorial–Cardozo station,
take the yellow or green line
to the Archives–Navy
Memorial–Penn Quarter
station and walk five blocks
west on Pennsylvania Ave.

Map labels: Drinks & Dinner on 14th St. — ⑤ · 14TH ST. · LAFAYETTE SQUARE · NEW YORK AVE. · G ST. · White House · Nightcap at the Hamilton ⑦ · F ST. · 21ST ST. · 20TH ST. · 19TH ST. · 18TH ST. · Bliss Out at the W ④ · F ST. · E ST. · NEW YORK AVE. · E ST. N.W. · W Washington D.C. Hotel · E ST. · AVENUE · D ST. · 17TH ST. · 15TH ST. · 14TH ST. · PENNSYLVANIA AVE. N.W. · 9TH ST. · C ST. N.W. · THE ELLIPSE · The Capitol Steps ⑥ · Federal Triangle · Archives–Navy Memorial–Penn Quarter · 20TH ST. · SOUTH PLACE · 12TH ST. · 10TH ST. · 7TH ST. · CONSTITUTION ① ⑤⓪ AVENUE

④ Bliss Out at the W (see p. 29) Pamper
yourself head to toe—complete with gratis
brownie bites—at the spa at the W Washington
D.C. hotel. Then walk seven blocks east to the
Gallery Place–Chinatown Metro station and take
the green or yellow line to the U St.–African-
American Civil War Memorial–Cardozo station;
from here, walk two blocks west on U St., N.W.

Georgetown Shopping

1 Begin with brunch at **Peacock Café** (*3251 Prospect St., N.W., tel 202-625-2740*), beloved for its eggs Benedict, French toast, and omelets. Then poke into shops along the picturesque brick sidewalks of M Street and Wisconsin Avenue, N.W., including **The Shops at Georgetown Park** (*3222 M St., N.W., tel 202-965-1280*).

Lunch at Washington Harbour

2 Restaurants spangle this popular riverfront area, ideal for strolling and, with plenty of benches, for people-watching too. **Sequoia** (*3000 K St., N.W., tel 202-944-4200*) is a bustling lunch venue, featuring American entrées, sandwiches, and salads—on a sunny day, ask for a table on the shady terrace overlooking the river.

Kayak or Bike on the Potomac

3 The nearby **Thompson Boat Center** (*2900 Virginia Ave., N.W., tel 202-333-9543, thompsonboatcenter.com*) offers

WHIRLWIND TOURS

M Street favorite Georgetown Cupcake has found nationwide fame on television.

hour-long kayak rentals—hop aboard and begin paddling around **Theodore Roosevelt Island,** or beneath nearby **Key Bridge,** for a different take on the Capital City. If you prefer cycling, rent two wheels from **Capital Bikeshare** (*capitalbikeshare.com*)—there's a depot near Waters Alley—and take a spin on the paths edging both sides of the Potomac while enjoying sublime views of the monuments.

Bliss Out at the W

4 Late afternoon is the perfect time to pamper yourself, and the mod W Washington D.C. hotel's Bliss day spa is the ideal place to indulge. Whether you opt for the ginger rub massage or triple oxygen treatment, complimentary brownie bites are obligatory.

515 15th St., N.W. • tel 202-661-2416 • blissworld.com • Metro: Metro Center

Drinks & Dinner on 14th Street

5 See pp. 132–133.

The Capitol Steps

6 Sit back for some political-inspired laughs with this hilarious musical extravaganza focusing on the topics of the day.

Ronald Reagan Building, 1300 Pennsylvania Ave., N.W. • tel 202-312-1555 • capsteps.com • Fri.–Sat. only • $$$$$ • Metro: Metro Center

Nightcap at the Hamilton

7 Relaxing at the British-style pub tucked away on the second floor of this cavernous bar/eatery is the perfect way to end a day of fun.

600 14th St., N.W. • tel 202-787-1000 • thehamiltondc.com • Metro: Metro Center

IN **THE KNOW**

Washington, D.C., was devastated by riots after Martin Luther King's assassination in 1968. But beginning with **Penn Quarter** in the late 1990s and **U Street** and **14th Street** after that, one neighborhood after the next is being revitalized. Northeast's **H Street** is fast becoming the place to enjoy a night out. **The Yards,** east of Nationals Park, is also thriving. Now it's the **Southwest Waterfront's** turn, with a huge redevelopment plan bringing restaurants, a movie theater, clubs, bars, and a concert hall along the Washington Channel.

WHIRLWIND TOURS

D.C. With Kids

Zoo animals, monsters, and spies are just some
of Washington's offerings for kids.

❶ Start Your Day With the Animals (see p. 32) Start your day watching the animals wake at the National Zoological Park. Walk 1 mile (1.6 km) west on Cathedral Ave., N.W.

❷ Hunt for Gargoyles (see p. 32) Find Darth Vader, a fanged snake, and more among the gargoyles on the Washington National Cathedral. Then take a taxi or walk 1.3 miles (2 km) up Wisconsin Ave., N.W., to the Tenleytown–AU Metro station; take the red line to the Gallery Place–Chinatown station.

GEORGE WASHINGTON MEM. PKWY.

VA.
MD.

MD.
D.C.

Tenleytown–AU

WESTERN AVE.

WISCONSIN AVE.

CONNECTICUT AVE.

MILITARY RD.

GLOVER ARCHBOLD PARK

MASSACHUSETTS AVE.

Washington National Cathedral

Hunt for Gargoyles ❷

Start Your Day With the Animals ❶

National Zoological Park

Woodley Park–Zoo–Adams Morgan

ROCK CREEK PARK

Rock Creek

16TH ST.

GEORGIA AVE.

7TH ST.

NEW HAMPSHIRE AVE.

N.W. | N.E.

NORTH CAPITOL ST.

RHODE ISLAND AVE.

NEW YORK AVE.

EASTERN AVE.

D.C.
MD.

29

1

30

U.S. NATIONAL ARBORETUM

ANACOSTIA RIVER PARK

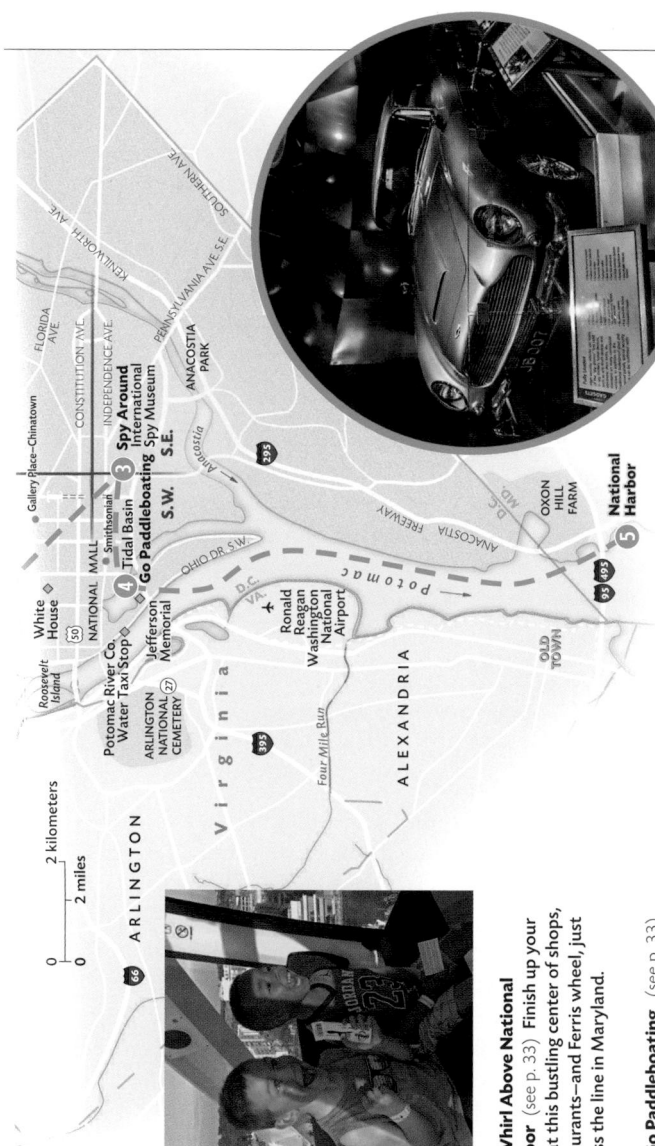

⑤ Whirl Above National Harbor (see p. 33) Finish up your day at this bustling center of shops, restaurants—and Ferris wheel, just across the line in Maryland.

④ Go Paddleboating (see p. 33) Tootle around the Tidal Basin for a waterborne view of the Jefferson Memorial and the famous cherry trees—beautiful even when they're not in bloom. Take the Potomac River Company water taxi from Ohio Dr., S.W., to National Harbor.

③ Spy Around (see pp. 32, 105) Visit the International Spy Museum—and/or embark on a neighborhood spy tour. Next walk south on L'Enfant Plaza; cross Maine Ave., S.W., and walk west.

D.C. WITH KIDS   DISTANCE: 4 MILES (6.4 KM)   TIME: APPROX. 8 HOURS   METRO: WOODLEY PARK–ZOO–ADAMS MORGAN

Start Your Day With the Animals

1 Explore the National Zoological Park early in the morning before the crowds descend—and when the animals are starting their day. The gates open at 6 a.m., prime time to watch the red pandas, lionesses, and gibbons play, cavort, and run about. (Arrive early to avoid long lines to see the famous giant pandas.)

3001 Connecticut Ave., N.W. • tel 202-633-4888 • nationalzoo.si.edu • Metro: Woodley Park–Zoo–Adams Morgan

Hunt for Gargoyles

2 The Gothic-style Washington National Cathedral ranks as the world's sixth largest cathedral, utilizing 30 million pounds of Indiana limestone and the talent of five architects and thousands of masons, sculptors, and other workers over 83 years (finishing in 1990). Kids love the "Gargoyle Tour," focusing on the fantastical and imaginary creatures and people serving as rainspouts on its exterior.

3101 Wisconsin Ave., N.W. • tel 202-537-6200 • cathedral .org • Gargoyle Tour: May–September only • $$ • Metro: Tenleytown–AU, then Bus: 31, 32, 36, or 37 south (or walk 1.5 miles/2.4 km down Wisconsin Ave.)

IN **THE KNOW**

Museums throughout D.C. have special sections and fun activities just for kids, such as the **National Building Museum** (see p. 94), with hands-on building activities. At the **National Museum of Natural History** (see p. 56) an interactive learning experience called Q?rius helps kids understand science as it relates to nature and their lives. The Smithsonian's Ripley Center's **Discovery Theater** (1100 Jefferson Dr., S.W., tel 202-633-8700, discoverytheater.org) focuses on art, science, and heritage.

Spy Around

3 (See p. 105) After getting their own secret identity, kids (and adults) set out to test their skills at the interactive International Spy Museum. You'll slide through an air-conditioning duct to spy on people below; test your observation, analysis, and disguise skills; and learn the stories behind spycraft. Gadgets galore (mostly from the '50s and '60s) add to the allure. A special "Spies in the City Experience" involves a mission assignment and hunting for clues around Washington.

700 L'Enfant Plaza, S.W. • tel 202-393-7798 • spymuseum.org • $$$$ adults, $$$ kids • Metro: Smithsonian

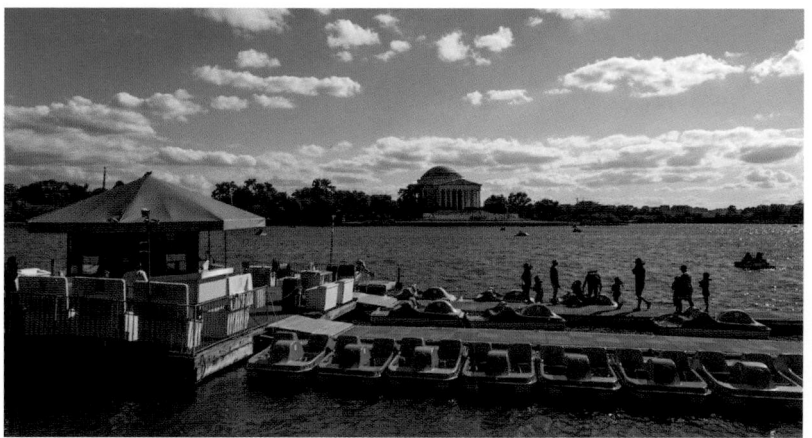

Paddleboating on the Tidal Basin is a cool way to beat the Washington heat.

Go Paddleboating

4 Let the kids work off their extra energy while viewing the Jefferson Memorial, Martin Luther King, Jr. Memorial, and the cherry trees from a waterborne perspective on the Tidal Basin.

1501 Maine Ave., S.W. • tel 202-479-2426 • tidalbasinpaddleboats.com • Kids need to have an adult onboard • $$$ • Metro: Smithsonian

Whirl Above National Harbor

5 Take a Potomac River water taxi from Ohio Drive *(tel 703-684-0580 or 877-511-2628, potomacriverboatco.com)* to **National Harbor,** a thriving waterfront commercial center with restaurants, shops, and Gaylord National Resort. Overshadowing it all is the giant **Capital Wheel** *(116 Waterfront St., National Harbor, MD, tel 301-842-8650, thecapitalwheel.com, $$$)*—a big Ferris wheel that sweeps you 180 feet (55 m) into the air for magnificent views in all directions. Kids can point out the White House, U.S. Capitol, and, far off in the distance, Arlington National Cemetery. A nearby carousel offers rides on whimsical and wild animals.

African-American Heritage

Discover the legacies of some of the greatest—and lesser known—
African Americans in Washington and beyond.

❶ Martin Luther King, Jr. Memorial (see pp. 36, 54) Pay homage to the leader of the civil rights movement at his memorial on the Tidal Basin. Walk east on Independence Ave., S.W., and north on 15th St., S.W./N.W.

❷ National Museum of African American History and Culture (see p. 36) Devote as much time as you can to this museum celebrating the African-American legacy in the U.S. From the Archives–Navy Memorial–Penn Quarter Metro station, take the green line to the Anacostia station and walk 0.75 mile (1.2 km). Go right on Howard Rd., S.E., left on Martin Luther King, Jr. Ave., S.E., and right on W St., S.E.

MAP A

CONSTITUTION AVE.

17TH ST.

National Museum of African American History and Culture ❷

Washington Monument

National WWII Memorial

Reflecting Pool

To Archives-Navy Memorial-PennQuarter Metro station

Lincoln Memorial

Korean War Veterans Memorial

D.C. WWI Veterans Mem.

INDEPENDENCE AVENUE

OHIO DRIVE

WEST BASIN DRIVE

KUTZ BRIDGE

❶ **Martin Luther King, Jr. Memorial**

RAOUL WALLENBERG PL.

14TH STREET N.W.

Tidal Basin

Tidal Basin Boat House

Washington, D.C.

Md.

N.W. | **N.E.**

AREAS C
ENLARGED

A S.W. S.E.

Potomac

Anacostia

Virginia

B

Md.

Japanese Cherry Trees

Franklin Delano Roosevelt Memorial

0 —— 400 meters
0 —— 400 yards

Jefferson Memorial

1

AFRICAN-AMERICAN HERITAGE   DISTANCE: 4.3 MILES (6.9 KM)
TIME: APPROX. 10 HOURS   METRO: SMITHSONIAN

MAP C

Lincoln Theatre

Ben's Chili Bowl

V ST.

U ST. N.W.

U Street–African-Amer Civil War Museum–Cardozo

African American Civil War Memorial and Museum ⑤

FLORIDA AVE

14TH ST.

13TH ST.

11TH ST.

VERMONT AVE

9TH ST.

7TH ST.

Shaw–Howard

S ST.

R ST.

RHODE ISLAND AVE

Q ST.

P ST.

Logan Circle

0   0.25 kilometers

0   0.25 miles

⑥ Lincoln Theatre (see p. 37)
Round out your day with a show at the famed 1920s theater and music club.

⑤ African American Civil War Memorial and Museum (see p. 37) Visit another Smithsonian-affiliated museum, this one focusing on the African-American role in the Civil War. Walk two blocks east on U St., N.W.

MAP B

❸ Frederick Douglass National Historic Site (see p. 36) Visit the last home of the sage of Anacostia. Walk 1 mile (1.6 km) west via Morris Rd., S.E.

Washington Channel

Nationals Park

Navy Yard–Ballpark

M ST. N.E.

SOUTHEAST BLVD.

Anacostia

Washington Navy Yard

10TH ST. S.E.

11TH ST. BRIDGE

ANACOSTIA PARK

NAYLOR RD.

OFFICER KEVIN J. WELSH MEMORIAL BRIDGE

295

16TH ST. S.E.

MINN. AVE

22ND ST.

S ST. S.E.

S CAPITOL ST. S.W.

S.W. | S.E.

GOOD HOPE ROAD S.E.

❹ Anacostia Community Museum (see p. 37) This Smithsonian-affiliated museum has fascinating exhibits related to the African-American experience in D.C. Backtrack 1.2 miles (1.9 km) via Morris Rd., S.E., to the Anacostia Metro station and take the green line to the U St.–African-American Civil War Memorial–Cardozo station.

HOWARD ROAD

LUTHER KING JR. AVE

14TH ST.

W STREET

Anacostia

MARTIN

MORRIS RD.

SHERIDAN RD.

STANTON

HUNTER PLACE

HUNTER RD.

Frederick Douglass National Historic Site ❸

FORT STANTON PARK

BRUCE PL.

Anacostia Community Museum ❹

0   400 meters

0   400 yards

WHIRLWIND TOURS

Martin Luther King, Jr. Memorial

1 (See p. 54) This granite monument honors Dr. King's dedication and perseverance in fighting for civil rights. Take time to read some of his most famous, and discerning, quotes. Then walk over to the **Lincoln Memorial,** where a plaque marks the step where King stood to give his famous "I Have a Dream" speech in 1963.

1964 Independence Ave., S.W. • tel 202-426-6841 • nps.gov/mlkm
• Metro: Smithsonian

National Museum of African American History and Culture

2 This new Smithsonian museum celebrates African-American heritage in the nation's capital from the Civil War and beyond. Don't miss the **"Black Fashion Collection,"** the **"Ernest C. Withers Photography Collection,"** and the **"Harriet Tubman Collection."**

1400 Constitution Ave., N.W. • tel 844-750-3012 • nmaahc.si.edu
• Metro: Smithsonian

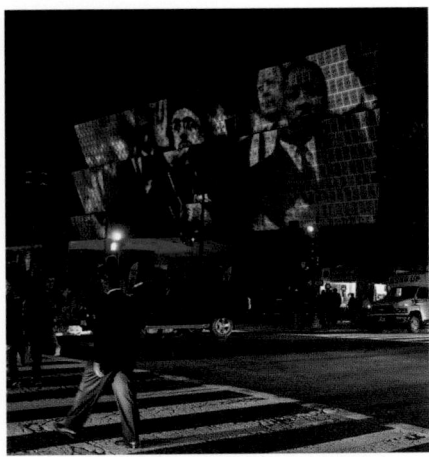

The building itself is a canvas at the National Museum of African American History and Culture.

Frederick Douglass National Historic Site

3 Born a slave, Frederick Douglass bought his freedom and became an important contributor to the civil rights movement. His grand hilltop house contains more than 70 percent of the Douglass family belongings, including the leader's favorite chair, his eyeglasses, and his walking stick. The house can only be seen by a guided tour—reserve ahead online.

1411 W St., S.E. • tel 202-426-5961
• nps.gov/frdo • By guided tour only
• $ (admin. fee) • Metro: Anacostia

Anacostia Community Museum

4 Temporary exhibits examine the history and culture of the predominantly African-American Anacostia neighborhood and beyond, featuring the works of local artists and thought leaders. Examples in the past have included "How the Civil War Changed Washington," "Separate and Unequaled: Black Baseball in the District of Columbia," and "Twelve Years that Shook and Shaped Washington: 1963–1975."

1901 Fort Place, S.E. • tel 202-633-4820 • anacostia.si.edu • Metro: Anacostia

African American Civil War Memorial and Museum

5 Newspaper articles, uniforms, weapons, and more honor African-American contributions to the Civil War in this museum. "Better even to die free than to live slaves," uttered Frederick Douglass—his words captured in bronze upon a **sculpture** across the street, honoring the African-American troops who fought in the Union Army.

Memorial: U St. & Vermont Ave., N.W. • Museum: 1925 Vermont Ave., N.W. • tel 202-667-2667 • Museum: closed Sun morning • afroamcivilwar.org • Metro: U St.–African-American Civil War Memorial–Cardozo

Lincoln Theatre

6 End your walking tour with a theater, dance, or comedy show at this legendary movie palace and live-performance venue, dating from 1922. Back in the day, luminaries taking to the stage ranged from Washington natives Duke Ellington and Pearl Bailey to Cab Calloway, Ella Fitzgerald, and Sarah Vaughan.

1215 U St., N.W. • tel 202-888-0050 or 877-435-9849 • thelincolndc.com; check website for performances • Metro: U St.–African-American Civil War Memorial–Cardozo

IN **THE KNOW**

Mr. Henry's may be a popular Capitol Hill burger spot, but it's also a famed venue in the annals of jazz history. Powerhouse Roberta Flack honed her skills here in the 1960s, R&B singers Donny Hathaway and Julia Nixon frequented the joint in the mid-1980s, and local post-bop trumpeter Kevin Cordt arrived in the early 2000s. Recently, jazz has returned on Friday nights, with other music slated throughout the week. *601 Pennsylvania Ave., S.E., tel 202-546-8412, mrhenrysdc.com*

Embassy Row

Peek into the diplomatic side of the Capital City along Massachusetts Avenue, N.W. —aka Embassy Row, where many of the world's diplomatic missions are clustered— and see how many national flags you can identify flying out in front.

8 Washington National Cathedral (see p. 41) Absorb the immensity of the National Cathedral then rest your weary feet at its Open City café.

7 Observatory Circle (see p. 41) The vice president of the United States—and the Naval Observatory—reside behind this circle's high iron fence. Continue up Massachusetts, turning right onto Wisconsin Ave, N.W.

6 Embassy of South Africa (see p. 41) A statue of Nelson Mandela means your long walk has brought you to the South Africa embassy. Continue up Massachusetts Ave, N.W.

1 Dupont Circle (see pp. 40, 130–131) Begin your walk at this fountain-graced circle, hub of the neighborhood. Then head up Massachusetts Ave., N.W.

2 Embassy of Indonesia (see p. 40) You can't miss the statue of Saraswati in front of this embassy near Dupont Circle. Cross Massachusetts Ave. and continue up its eastern side about 0.25 mile (0.4 km).

3 Sheridan Circle (see p. 40) Several embassies cluster around this circle with its statue of the Union general. Continue up Massachusetts Ave, staying on the street's eastern side.

4 Islamic Center of Washington (see p. 40) One of the oldest mosques in the U.S., where more than 6,000 pray on Fridays. Cross the Massachusetts Avenue Bridge, and continue northwest.

5 Embassy of Brazil (see p. 41) This modern embassy resembles a tinted glass cube on stilts. Continue up Massachusetts Ave., N.W.

EMBASSY ROW DISTANCE: 2.3 MILES (3.7 KM)
TIME: APPROX. 2 HOURS   METRO: DUPONT CIRCLE

Map labels: ADAMS MORGAN · FLORIDA AVE · COLUMBIA RD · KALORAMA RD · 18TH ST · 19TH ST · R ST · Q ST · P ST · Dupont Circle · CONNECTICUT AVE · CALIFORNIA ST · S ST · 23RD ST · Kalorama Circle · 24TH ST · Sheridan Circle · MASSACHUSETTS AVENUE · Islamic Center of Washington · ROCK CREEK POTOMAC PKWY · Rock Creek · WHITEHAVEN ST · MASS AVE · BRIDGE · Embassy of Brazil · Embassy of South Africa · Embassy of Indonesia · 0 200 meters · 0 200 yards

WHIRLWIND TOURS

Dupont Circle

1 (See pp. 130–131) Begin the walk up Massachusetts Avenue—aka Embassy Row—at this graceful fountain featuring allegorical figures representing the sea, wind, and stars, and Civil War naval hero Samuel Francis du Pont.

Intersection of Connecticut Ave., Massachusetts Ave., P St., 19th St., *&* New Hampshire Ave., N.W. • Metro: Dupont Circle

Embassy of Indonesia

2 Evalyn Walsh McLean, the last private owner of the Hope Diamond, lived in this lavish 1903 mansion built by her father on profits made in Colorado gold mining. She sold it to the Republic of Indonesia in 1951.

2020 Massachusetts Ave., N.W. • private • Metro: Dupont Circle

Sheridan Circle

3 Ringed by a **dozen embassies, including Greece, Ireland,** and **Romania,** this circle hosts a statue of Union Civil War general Philip Sheridan sculpted by Gutzon Borglum.

Massachusetts Ave., N.W., at 23rd St., N.W. • Metro: Dupont Circle

Islamic Center of Washington

4 A 162-foot (49 m) minaret rises above what was once the Western Hemisphere's largest mosque. Visitors are free to enter; women must wear a scarf, and shoes must be removed.

2551 Massachusetts Ave., N.W. • tel 202-332-8343 • theislamiccenter.com • Metro: Dupont Circle

A statue of the Hindu goddess Saraswati rises outside the Embassy of Indonesia.

Embassy of Brazil

5 All glass and angles, the modernist Brazilian Embassy was designed by Brazilian architect Olavo Redig de Campos in the 1970s.

3006 Massachusetts Ave., N.W. • tel 202-238-2700 • private • Metro: Dupont Circle, Woodley Park–Zoo–Adams Morgan

Embassy of South Africa

6 You can't miss the South African embassy, with its large statue of Nelson Mandela, where sit-ins and protests took place to free him from prison and to end apartheid. Across the street a statue of Winston Churchill flashes his signature "V-for-victory" sign at the **British Embassy.**

3051 Massachusetts Ave., N.W. • tel 202-232-4400 • private • Metro: Dupont Circle, Woodley Park–Zoo–Adams Morgan

Observatory Circle

7 A ship anchor and the digital USNO Master Clock mark tree-shaded Observatory Circle, home to the **U.S. Naval Observatory** and the residence of the vice president of the United States. Among the embassies clustered around the circle, the modern **Embassy of Finland** (*3301 Massachusetts Ave., N.W., tel 202-298-5800*) has a cantilevered glass back wall projected over Rock Creek Park. It's open occasionally for exhibitions, as well as special concerts.

Massachusetts Ave., N.W., bet. 30th & 34th Sts., N.W. • Metro: Dupont Circle, Woodley Park–Zoo–Adams Morgan

Washington National Cathedral

8 End your walk with some contemplative time at the world's sixth largest cathedral. Then rest your feet and enjoy a cup of coffee at the **Open City at the National Cathedral** café in the Old Baptistry.

3101 Wisconsin Ave., N.W. • tel 202-537-6200 • cathedral.org • $$ to visit cathedral Mon.–Sat., worshippers enter for free • Metro: Woodley Park–Zoo–Adams Morgan

SAVVY **TRAVELER**

If you're not a diplomat, the best way to get a peek inside D.C.'s beautifully decorated embassies is with the popular **"Around the World Embassy Tour"** in May, when some 50 diplomatic missions open their doors to guests with all kinds of programmed events. It's part of the month-long, citywide **Passport DC** program, with more than 100 globally inspired experiences. *culturaltourismdc.org*

WHIRLWIND TOURS

Downtown Georgetown's M Street

PART 2

Washington's Neighborhoods

Washington's Neighborhoods

Dupont Circle & Beyond **126**

ADAMS MORGAN

CONNECTICUT AVE

COLUMBIA ROAD

U STREET

STREET

18TH

SHERIDAN CIRCLE

MASSACHUSETTS

Dupont Circle

DUPONT CIRCLE

NEW HAMPSHIRE AVE

P ST.

RHODE

MONTROSE PARK

Rock Creek

WISCONSIN AVENUE

30TH STREET N.W.

31ST STREET

Q STREET

GEORGETOWN

Georgetown **142**

Georgetown University

M STREET NW

ROCK CREEK AND POTOMAC PKWY

White House & Around **106**

CHESAPEAKE AND OHIO CANAL NATIONAL HISTORICAL PARK

Chesapeake & Ohio Canal

WHITEHURST FREEWAY

NEW BRIDGE

Potomac

K STREET

25TH ST.

PENNSYLVANIA AVE.

Farragut North

Farragut West

LAFAYETTE SQUARE

FOGGY BOTTOM

H STREET

H ST.

I ST.

22ND STREET

23RD STREET

M ST.

17TH STREET

Roosevelt Island

Kennedy Center

66

Virginia

F ST.

21ST ST.

STREET

E STREET

23RD ST. N.W.

AVENUE

18TH

19TH

THEODORE ROOSEVELT MEMORIAL BRIDGE

C STREET

CONSTITUTION AVE.

Old Town Alexandria **158**

PENDLETON STREET

PRINCESS ST.

KING ST.

HENRY ST.

FAIRFAX ST.

DUKE ST.

WASHINGTON ST.

ROYAL ST.

PITT ST.

ST. ASAPH ST.

LEE ST.

UNION ST.

Market Square

WATERFRONT PARK

CAMERON ST.

NORTHWEST

SOUTHWEST

Lincoln Memorial

Reflecting Pool

WEST POTOMAC PARK

National WWII Memorial

ARLINGTON MEMORIAL BRIDGE

INDEPENDENCE AVE.

Potomac

OHIO

DRIVE

Tidal Basin

Jefferson Memorial

| 0 | 200 meters |
| 0 | 200 yards |

National Mall

NATIONAL MALL

Graced with world-class museums, marble monuments, and green spaces made for strolling, picnicking, and tossing a Frisbee, the nation's playground is a 2-mile-long (3 km), tree-shaded expanse first envisioned by architect Pierre-Charles L'Enfant in 1791. His original grandiose vision included stately residences along a "vast esplanade," a plan revised by the end of the 1800s for financial reasons. No worries—the National Mall, anchored by the Capitol at one end and the Lincoln Memorial at the other—does not disappoint. Indeed, here is where you'll find the celebrated Smithsonian museums (all free of charge), including the ever popular National Air and Space Museum and the National Museum of American History. Here, too, between 14th Street, N.W., and the Potomac River, are a string of majestic monuments to national heroes such as George Washington, Abraham Lincoln, and Thomas Jefferson, set alongside memorials to times of sacrifice such as World War II. You could spend a week—if not a month—exploring and still not see everything. Pace yourself!

48 Neighborhood Walk

58 In Depth: National Museum of American History

60 In Depth: National Air & Space Museum

64 Distinctly D.C.: Cherry Blossoms

66 Best Of: Free Entertainment

❶ **The Mall is the capital's premier public park, peppered with monuments and museums.**

National Mall

Plan a full day to explore the country's most significant collection of museums and monuments on the National Mall—dubbed America's Front Yard.

❸ Vietnam Veterans Memorial (see pp. 51–52) Shocking when first unveiled in 1982, this minimalistic, black-granite memorial has become one of the nation's most revered. Go southwest, to the end of the Reflecting Pool.

❷ National World War II Memorial (see p. 51) A graceful, waterfall-centered memorial to the heroes of the "Greatest Generation." Continue west through Constitution Gardens just north of the Reflecting Pool.

❶ Washington Monument (see p. 50) The nation's 555-foot (169 m) marble tribute to the first president. Walk west, crossing 17th St., N.W.

❹ Lincoln Memorial (see pp. 52–53) The imposing statue of a seated Lincoln deep in contemplation draws some six million visitors each year. Follow the pathway just to the southeast.

NATIONAL MALL

❺ Korean War Veterans Memorial (see pp. 53) One of the Mall's more hidden memorials, yet every bit as potent as the others in its declaration that freedom is not free. Walk southeast toward the Tidal Basin, crossing Independence Ave., S.W., at the second traffic light.

NATIONAL MALL   DISTANCE: 4.1 MILES (6.6 KM)
TIME: 8 HOURS   METRO START: SMITHSONIAN

⑪ National Gallery of Art
(see pp. 56–57) Experience this remarkable collection of world-famous masters in two parts—the classical West Building and the modern East Building. Then head across the National Mall.

⑫ National Air and Space Museum (see pp. 60–63) One of the planet's most visited museums, celebrating the air and space revolutions through the ages.

⑩ National Museum of Natural History (see p. 56) Marvel at the mammoth elephant, the Hope Diamond, a real-life coral reef, and more. Then walk east.

⑨ National Museum of American History (see pp. 58–59) A tribute to American history and culture: Julia Child's kitchen, the first ladies' gowns, the Star-Spangled Banner—they're all here. Continue east on the National Mall to the next big building between 12th and 9th Sts., N.W.

NATIONAL MALL

⑥ Martin Luther King, Jr. Memorial (see p. 54) The 30-foot (9 m) likeness of the civil rights leader symbolically emerges from the Stone of Hope. Follow the pathway south of the memorial, along the Tidal Basin.

⑦ Franklin Delano Roosevelt Memorial (see pp. 54–55) Four separate outdoor granite alcoves represent the 32nd president's four terms in office. Continue to the Tidal Basin's south side.

⑧ Thomas Jefferson Memorial (see p. 55) This neoclassical temple celebrates the innovative third president. Continue around the Tidal Basin to Raoul Wallenberg Place, S.W., which becomes 15th St., N.W.; turn right at Madison Dr.

Washington Monument

1 Soaring above D.C.'s low skyline and surrounded by American flags representing every state, this 555-foot-5.9-inch (169 m) spire honors America's first president. Begun in 1848, the iconic marble-and-granite obelisk sat half finished between 1854 and 1879 due to a design disagreement, lack of funding, and the Civil War. At long last the monument was dedicated in 1885; the change of stone color about 150 feet (46 m) above the base marks where work resumed with stone from a different quarry. While no longer the world's tallest man-made structure, it remains the world's tallest obelisk. To go up, free, timed tickets are available at the monument's base (or reserve them online at *recreation.gov*). A 60-second elevator ride ascends to vast views over the city. On the descent the elevator slows down, allowing you to see the change in old and new marble from the inside, as well as commemorative stones and inscriptions.

2 15th St., N.W. • tel 202-426-6841 • nps.gov/wamo • tickets: tel 877-444-6777 or recreation.gov • Metro: Smithsonian

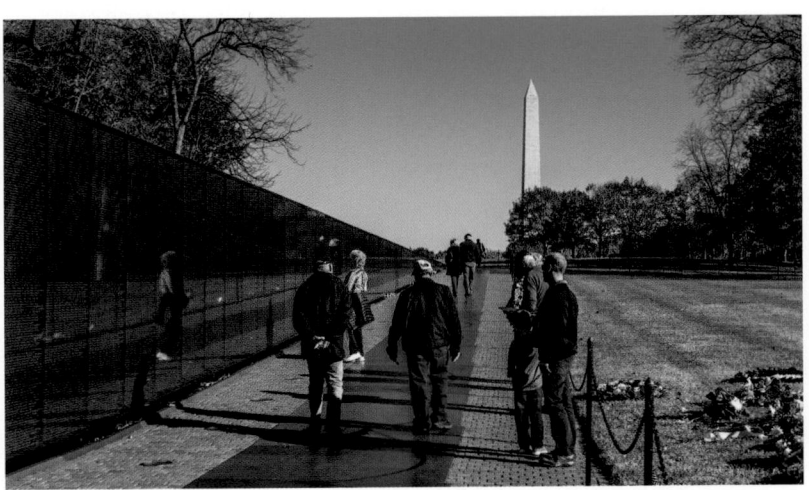

Descending walls of the Vietnam Veterans Memorial reflect the memories of those who served.

National World War II Memorial

2 A graceful, fountain-spouting pool encircled by columns and arches comprises this sober memorial to the 16.1 million soldiers who served the nation during World War II—and honors those who gave the ultimate sacrifice. Look closer, and you'll begin to understand the symbolism. The **Freedom Wall** with 4,048 gold stars pays tribute to the more than 400,000 Americans killed during the conflict (each star represents 100 American military deaths). Arcing out from there, 56 granite pillars stand for each U.S. state and federal territory (and the District of Columbia) involved in the war. They're arranged based on each one's entry date into the Union, starting with Delaware to the right of the Freedom Wall, followed by Pennsylvania to the left, with the order alternating north to south. The 43-foot-high (13 m) arches anchoring the columns symbolize the war's Atlantic and Pacific theaters. In addition, two dozen bronze panels depict scenes from the war. Every war veteran will recognize the two "Kilroy Was Here" drawings hidden in the memorial. These mimic the popular cartoon image of a man looking over a wall, graffiti often left by servicemen to indicate they had passed through an area. If you have time, search the computerized registry for a family member or friend you know who served in the war—both overseas and on the home front.

17th St. & Independence Ave., N.W. • tel 202-426-6841 or 800-639-4WW2 • nps.gov/wwii • Metro: Smithsonian

SAVVY **TRAVELER**

The Smithsonian Institution, established in 1846, comprises a total of 19 museums, 9 research centers, and the National Zoo—with 11 museums on the Mall. Visit the website for an overview, or stop by **The Castle,** which offers a visitor center and planning map, as well as mini displays on each museum to help you decide where to go. *1000 Jefferson Dr., S.W., tel 202-633-1000, si.edu*

Vietnam Veterans Memorial

3 Designed by Maya Lin and dedicated in 1982, the distinctive Vietnam Veterans Memorial is a startling modern contrast to the ode to classicism of the monuments surrounding it. Two 246-foot-long (75 m) walls create a black-granite wedge cutting into the earth, symbolically representing a wound that has closed and is

NATIONAL MALL

IN **THE KNOW**

When we use the term "National Mall," we typically mean the entire 2-mile-long (3 km) monument- and museum-dotted swath of parkland between the Lincoln Memorial in the west and the U.S. Capitol building in the east. In reality, this is wrong. The official National Mall occupies the land between the grounds of the U.S. Capitol and the Washington Monument. So what lies west of that? The land holding all of the monuments and memorials between the Washington Monument and the Lincoln Memorial is officially called West Potomac Park.

healing. The names of 58,307 Americans are etched into the glistening wall—a diamond marks those who died in action, while a cross indicates those missing in action. As you walk along the memorial, the wall becomes taller as the number of names increases, reaching a high point of 10.1 feet (3 m). You'll also notice how the granite's sheen reflects the images of visitors—including yourself—seemingly projecting life as much as honoring death. Piles of mementos from loved ones are left daily—medals, teddy bears, and at least one motorcycle; items are collected by the National Park Service and cataloged and stored. Nearby, a bronze statue titled "The Three Servicemen" puts faces to the names. Another bronze group called the "Vietnam Women's Memorial," added in 1993, honors the women who participated in the war. If you're looking for a specific name, use the Directory of Names, located at both ends of the wall and arranged alphabetically.

North side of Lincoln Memorial, near intersection of 22nd St. & Constitution Ave., N.W. • tel 202-426-6841 • nps.gov/vive • Metro: Foggy Bottom–GWU

Lincoln Memorial

4 Looking every bit like a classic Greek temple, the magnificent Lincoln Memorial, designed by Henry Bacon, honors the 16th president of the United States. The 36 fluted Doric columns represent the number of states in the Union at the time of Lincoln's death. Inside, at the top of the steps, you are greeted by the 19-foot-high (6 m) statue of a seated Lincoln, carved under the direction of Daniel Chester French in white Georgia marble. Lincoln's clenched left hand shows strength and resolve; his right hand lies open to signal compassion (it's an urban myth that he is signing "A.L."). Inspiring words from the Gettysburg Address and Lincoln's second

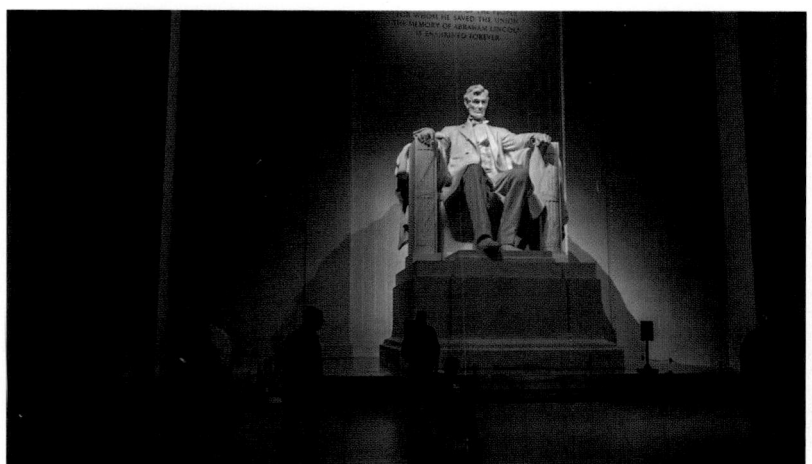

The gravitas of Abraham Lincoln's leadership is felt at his memorial, especially at night.

inaugural address are inscribed on the memorial's side chambers. Don't miss the display of Lincoln's writings and speeches on the lower level, where you can also watch a video on the site's long history of protests and demonstrations. Martin Luther King, Jr., delivered his famous "I Have a Dream" speech in front of the memorial in 1963; an engraved plaque marks the stair where he stood.

2 Lincoln Memorial Circle, N.W. • tel 202-426-6841 • nps.gov/linc • Metro: Foggy Bottom–GWU

Korean War Veterans Memorial

⑤ Nineteen larger-than-life, stainless-steel soldiers walk in formation through juniper bushes, a sea of photographic faces watching them from a granite wall. Dedicated in 1992, this moving memorial commemorates the 5.8 million Americans who served in the three-year conflict. Inscriptions on the **Pool of Remembrance** note the number of soldiers killed, wounded, MIA, and imprisoned as POWs.

900 Ohio Dr., S.W. • tel 202-426-6841 • nps.gov/kowa • Metro: Foggy Bottom–GWU

Martin Luther King, Jr. Memorial

6 Dedicated in 2011, this eye-catching memorial on the edge of the Tidal Basin honors the clergyman, activist, and nonviolence advocate who so diligently and poignantly advanced the civil rights movement both in the United States and around the world. Referencing his landmark "I Have a Dream" speech, King's 19-foot (6 m) likeness emerges from the rough-hewn Stone of Hope, beyond a boulder split in two representing the Mountain of Despair. After pondering the symbolism of your own figurative walk through the Mountain of Despair, take time to read some of King's most famous, and discerning, quotes etched into the adjacent 450-foot-long (137 m) inscription wall; the earliest dates from the 1955 Montgomery bus boycott in Alabama, the latest from King's last sermon, delivered in 1968 just a day before his assassination in Memphis.

1964 Independence Ave., S.W. • tel 202-426-6841 • nps.gov/mlkm
• Metro: Smithsonian

A detail from the five massive bronze canvases expressing the impact of FDR's social programs

Franklin Delano Roosevelt Memorial

7 Set on the Tidal Basin's west side, this striking, 7.5-acre (3 ha) memorial, opened in 1997, honors the 32nd president of the United States. It is also the only presidential memorial to include a first lady, as well as a first pet. Four unroofed, red-granite-walled alcoves—one for each of his four terms, between 1933 and 1945—spread along the water's edge. These mark Roosevelt's greatest struggles and triumphs, including the Depression, the New Deal, and World

War II. Stroll through the rooms, admiring the landscaped plazas, waterfalls, quiet pools, and statues, and reading the famous FDR quotations engraved on the walls, among them the inspiring words from his first inaugural address, "The only thing we have to fear is fear itself."

400 W. Basin Dr., S.W. • tel 202-426-6841 • nps.gov/frde • Metro: Smithsonian

Thomas Jefferson Memorial

8 Dedicated to the drafter of the Declaration of Independence and the third U.S. president, this graceful white-marble structure was designed by John Russell Pope in the style of the ancient Roman Pantheon and completed in 1943. Inside the colonnade building, a 19-foot (6 m) bronze statue of a stately Thomas Jefferson stands beneath a towering dome. Among the quotes on the wall is one from a letter written in 1800: "for I have sworn upon the altar of god eternal hostility against every form of tyranny over the mind of man." A lower lobby has exhibits, a gift shop, and a bookstore. From the front, you can't miss the iconic view of the Tidal Basin, with its twirling gulls and paddleboats and springtime cherry blossoms, the Washington Monument rising behind. Beyond that, in a deliberately straight line, rises the White House and all the symbolism of democracy that emanates from it.

13 E. Basin Dr., S.W. • tel 202-426-6841 • nps.gov/thje • Metro: Smithsonian

National Museum of American History

9 See pp. 58–59.

National Mall bet. 12th & 14th Sts., N.W. • tel 202-633-1000 • americanhistory.si.edu • Metro: Smithsonian, Federal Triangle

See pp. 58–59.

GOOD **EATS**

■ **GARDEN CAFÉ**
Artsy menus are coordinated with themed exhibits at the hosting National Gallery of Art in this West Building café. **National Mall bet. 4th & 7th Sts., N.W., tel 202-712-7454, $**

■ **MITSITAM CAFÉ**
Authentic indigenous cuisine of the Americas served cafeteria style within the National Museum of the American Indian. **950 Independence Ave., S.W., tel 202-633-1000, $$**

■ **PAVILION CAFÉ**
Sandwiches, soup, and salads with flair within the National Gallery of Art's lovely sculpture garden. **Bet. Madison Dr. & Constitution Ave., N.W., tel 202-289-3360, $$**

National Museum of Natural History

10 Entering the Rotunda from the Mall side of this enormous museum, you're greeted by an **African bush elephant,** 13 feet 2 inches (4 m) at the shoulder. You'd need all day to visit the rest of the museum, beginning on the first floor with a pass clockwise through the **Hall of Mammals,** with mounted animals from near and far; and the **Hall of Human Origins,** with representations of ancient paintings—handprints, animals, and the like—from around the world. This will lead you into the **Sant Ocean Hall,** with its 45-foot-long (14 m) model of an Atlantic right whale hanging from the ceiling and huge tank containing an Indo-Pacific coral reef alive with up to 74 fishes and other tropical denizens. You'll then pass through **African Voices**—an exploration of how African people have influenced global culture—and the **David H. Koch Hall of Fossils,** tracing Earth's 4.6 billion years of evolution, including a *T. rex* among its dinosaur skeletons. On the second floor, don't miss the dazzling, 45.52-carat **Hope Diamond,** perhaps the world's most famous precious stone. Also on this floor are the **Butterfly Pavilion** (*$$, free Tues.*) and **Live Insect Zoo.**

National Mall bet. 9th & 12th Sts., N.W. • tel 202-633-1000 • naturalhistory.si.edu • Metro: Smithsonian

National Gallery of Art

11 One of the world's finest repositories of Western art, the National Gallery is another must-see. The collection is housed in two distinct structures—the **West Building,** a classical pantheon with barrel-vaulted halls designed by John Russell Pope, showcasing masterpieces from the 13th to 19th centuries; and the modern **East Building,** designed by I. M. Pei, displaying works from the late 19th century onward. For those short on time and wanting to see the most famous paintings, begin in the West Building with the **Dutch works,** including Hendrick ter Brugghen's "Bagpipe Player" (1624; Gallery 44). Next up, the **Collection of Italian Art** with a portrait of Ginevra de'Benci (1474/1478; Gallery 06), the only painting by Leonardo

An African bush elephant greets visitors to the vast National Museum of Natural History, showcasing wonders of the natural world.

da Vinci on public view in North America. Next, savor the **French Impressionists,** including Claude Monet's "Woman With a Parasol" (1875; Gallery 85). Then move to the newly renovated East Building and such highlights of **modern art** as Andy Warhol's "Green Marilyn" (1962) and Andy Goldsworthy's "Roof" (2004–2005). Outside, the adjacent **National Gallery of Art Sculpture Garden** offers large installations displayed around a fountain in a lovely setting of trees and flowers. Free jazz concerts take place here on summer Friday evenings, and ice-skating in winter.

West Building: National Mall bet. 4th & 7th Sts., N.W.; East Building: National Mall bet. 3rd & 4th Sts., N.W. ; Sculpture Garden: National Mall bet. 7th & 8th Sts., N.W. • tel 202-737-4215 • nga.gov • Metro: Smithsonian

National Air and Space Museum
12 See pp. 60–63.
National Mall bet. 4th & 7th Sts., S.W. • tel 202-633-2214 • airandspace.si.edu • Metro: L'Enfant Plaza

National Museum of American History

Some of America's most iconic treasures celebrate everything from the president's role to the Star-Spangled Banner to screen legends in this homage to the nation's history and culture.

Michelle Obama revisits the white silk chiffon gown she wore to the 2009 Inaugural Ball, now part of the "First Ladies" exhibit at the National Museum of American History.

This artifact-filled museum applauds all things great in American history and culture, focusing on such broad themes as transportation, food, the president's role, and innovation. With more than three million items in its collection— as diverse and symbolic as Abraham's Lincoln's top hat, Thomas Edison's light bulbs, and Archie Bunker's armchair—only 3 to 5 percent is on display at any one time. Here are some not-to-be-missed highlights.

NATIONAL MALL

■ STAR-SPANGLED BANNER

Moved by the sight of the enormous garrison flag flying over Fort McHenry in Baltimore Harbor during the War of 1812, attorney and amateur poet Francis Scott Key scribbled the lyrics to what became the national anthem of the United States. Recently conserved, the same hallowed flag that he viewed is on permanent display as you enter the building from the Mall, on the second floor, with background information on its creator, Mary Pickersgill; the role of the flag in the American psyche; and how the flag was preserved.

■ DOROTHY'S RUBY SLIPPERS

The **American Stories** gallery on the second floor displays some of America's most iconic artifacts of pop culture, including the ruby slippers worn by Judy Garland in the 1939 movie *The Wizard of Oz*. Look also for the fragment of Plymouth Rock and the original Muppet puppets.

■ JACQUELINE KENNEDY'S STATE DINNER DRESS

Jackie's elegant yellow silk gown with an overlay of crepe chiffon, a gift from

IN **THE KNOW**

Recent renovation at the museum has sought to bring new relevancy to its interpretation of the American experience. Exhibits explore innovation, the past and present of American democracy, and the role of immigrants in the U.S. melting pot. On display are such prized possessions as Thomas Jefferson's writing desk, on which he wrote the Declaration of Independence.

designer Oleg Cassini, joins first ladies' dresses dating as far back as Martha Washington's silk gown from the early 1780s in the ever popular "First Ladies" exhibit on the third floor center level. In addition to the lovely dresses, the exhibit explores the first ladies' social and political activities.

■ JULIA CHILD'S KITCHEN

For seven years, in her Cambridge, Massachusetts home, Julia Child gave lessons, tested recipes, and cooked on national television in this very kitchen. In 2001, some 1,200 items and the kitchen were packed and reassembled here. You'll find it in the "FOOD: Transforming the American Table 1950–2000" exhibit on the first floor.

National Mall bet. 12th & 14th Sts, N.W. • tel 202-633-1000 • americanhistory.si.edu • Metro: Smithsonian, Federal Triangle

NATIONAL MALL

National Air & Space Museum

The evolution of air and space is explored in this magnificent, ever popular museum on the Mall.

Real aircraft are part of what attracts some 9 million visitors annually to this popular museum, celebrating humankind's achievements in aviation and spaceflight.

Celebrity air- and spacecraft, intriguing artifacts, interactive exhibits, state-of-the-art digital displays, and films all tell the story of our fascination with flight, from the earliest days of hot-air ballooning to the Wright brothers' experiments with gliders to the current exploration of space. In 2018, the museum, which spans topics from the science of flight to the concept of the universe, launched a seven-year renovation that will completely transform its 23 galleries.

The renovation will refresh some exhibitions but retain their current themes; others will be completely replaced, with the first galleries scheduled to reopen in 2022. Although the museum will remain open during the renovation, in 2019 nine exhibition halls closed. While many iconic artifacts will temporarily go off display, the following will remain on display for the next few years. Most are in the **Boeing Milestones of Flight Hall,** which highlights aviation's greatest hits just as you enter the museum from the Mall. The Hall is being reconfigured, including a stunning new entrance.

■ CHARLES LINDBERGH'S *SPIRIT OF ST. LOUIS*

Charles Lindbergh made the first non-stop solo flight across the Atlantic on May 20–21, 1927, in a custom-built single-engine, single-seat monoplane—*Spirit of St. Louis*—which hangs from the ceiling of the Boeing Milestones of Flight Hall. Lindbergh took off from Long Island, New York, and landed 33 hours, 30 minutes later in Paris, France, after flying 3,600 miles (5,800 km), thus winning the $25,000 Orteig Prize for the first transatlantic flight.

■ BELL X-1

Also suspended in the Boeing Milestones of Flight Hall is the orange, rocket-powered Bell X-1 "Glamorous Glennis," the first airplane to fly faster than the speed of sound. Piloted by Charles "Chuck" Yeager, on October 14, 1947, the X-1 was drop-launched from a B-29 and reached a speed of 700 mph (1,127 kph), Mach 1.06, at an altitude of 43,000 feet (13,000 m). On March 26, 1948, Yaeger took the X-1 to an altitude of 71,900 feet (21,900 m) and a speed of 957 mph (1,540 kph)—the highest altitude and velocity thus far attained by a manned aircraft.

■ APOLLO LUNAR MODULE

Rising on four stilt-legs from the floor of the Boeing Milestones of Flight Hall is an Apollo Lunar Module (LM)—the two-stage lander spacecraft designed to ferry two astronauts from lunar orbit to the Moon's surface and back. Built by Grumman Aircraft, the Smithsonian module (LM2) was used for ground testing prior to the first successful Moon-landing mission. Its descent stage has been modified to appear like the Apollo 11 Lunar Module "Eagle" flown by Neil Armstrong and Edwin "Buzz" Aldrin, Jr., for their historic 1969 landing.

■ MERCURY FRIENDSHIP 7

Adjacent to the Lunar Module is the

SAVVY **TRAVELER**

The largest and some of the most famous air- and spacecraft are displayed at the **Udvar-Hazy Center,** a huge Smithsonian annex in nearby Chantilly, Virginia. Here, in a hangar-like facility, you'll find more than 300 aircraft and large space objects, including the Boeing B-29 Superfortress *Enola Gay,* which dropped the first atomic bomb in combat; an Air France Concorde, the first supersonic airliner; and the space shuttle *Discovery,* fresh from its last flight. *14390 Air & Space Museum Pkwy., Chantilly, VA, tel 703-572-4118, airandspace.si.edu, parking: $$$*

NATIONAL MALL

bell-shaped capsule in which John Glenn became the first American to orbit the Earth, on February 20, 1962. Glenn's three-orbit mission as part of Project Mercury also involved the first reentry into Earth's atmosphere of a U.S.-manned flight. Note the scars on the convex heat shield! You can peer into the cramped interior through its single window. Glenn's flight lasted only 4 hours, 55 minutes, before he splashed down in the Atlantic.

■ 1903 WRIGHT FLYER
Examine up close the fabric-covered aircraft in which brothers Orville and Wilbur Wright inaugurated the aerial age with the world's first sustained flights of

a powered, heavier-than-air flying machine on December 17, 1903, at Kitty Hawk, North Carolina, culminating four years of trial and error using gliders. The Wright Flyer is displayed in the second floor's **Wright Brothers and the Invention of the Aerial Age Gallery,** which explores the first decade of flight. The Wright Flyer has skids instead of wheels for landing, plus a sprocket-and-chain transmission system—evidence of the Wrights' bicycle background.

■ NEIL ARMSTRONG'S APOLLO 11 SPACESUIT
In July 2019, Neil Armstrong's spacesuit worn during his "giant leap for mankind" following the historic Apollo 11 Moon landing in July 1969 was placed back on display for the first time in 13 years. Designed to thwart micrometeorites, radiation, extreme heat and cold, and tears from sharp rocks, the fragile suit is displayed in a state-of-the-art case in the **Wright Brothers** gallery, opposite the fabric and wood pieces of the Wright Flyer that Armstrong took with him to the Moon.

■ FLIGHT SIMULATORS
Climb inside a motion simulator and see for yourself what it's like to perform 360-degree barrel rolls, or test your skills at air-to-air combat in a F-4 Phantom II

Historic airplanes on display at the Smithsonian National Air and Space Museum

jet fighter. The simulators are in the Go Fly Zone, on the first floor at the museum's east end. Note that a fee is charged for each ride ($$).

■ IMAX Movies

The museum's popular IMAX theaters, complete with next-generation laser projection and sound systems, comfy seating, and enormous screens measuring up to six stories tall, are one of the museum's top highlights. For that reason, be sure to purchase tickets online ahead of time, or immediately upon entering the museum. Note that all shows charge an entrance fee ($$$).

600 Independence Ave., S.W. • tel 202- 633-2214 • airandspace.si.edu • Metro: L'Enfant Plaza

Cherry Blossoms

Every spring the city waits with bated breath for the blossoming of the famous, 3,000-plus Yoshino cherry trees along the Tidal Basin. It's never guaranteed exactly when they'll peak—April 4 is the average. But suddenly, seemingly overnight, everyone's mood notably lightens as these delicate little flowers, a gift from the Japanese in the early 20th century, explode into a billowy world of white and pink.

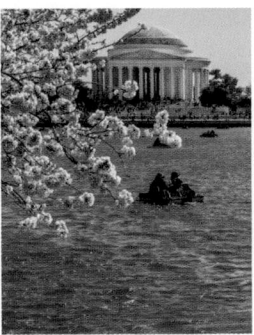

The undeniable seasonal beauty of masses of soft pink petals proves an irresistible draw for visitors to the Tidal Basin, whether viewed from the water (above) or beneath the boughs (opposite). The city's month-long festival honors the continuing friendship between the United States and Japan.

The First Trees

The idea for Washington's cherry trees can be traced to Eliza Scidmore, a late 19th-century travel writer who so admired the flowering cherry trees in Japan that she lobbied park officials to plant similar ones in her hometown of Washington, D.C. They weren't interested. About a quarter century later, botanist David Fairchild experimented with flowering cherry trees and planted some around the town of Chevy Chase, Maryland. These inspired First Lady Helen Taft to place some around a drab area along the Potomac River. In a gesture of friendship, the mayor of Tokyo, Japan, sent trees as a gift— twice, as the first arrived diseased. The second batch of 3,000 were planted along the Tidal Basin in March 1912, with Mrs. Taft placing the first one.

Blossom Viewing

The Japanese have turned *sakura* viewing into an art—called *hanami*—which involves long strolls as well as songs and picnics beneath the blooms. In D.C., visitors can experience hanami by paddleboat

NATIONAL MALL

(tidalbasinpaddleboats.com) for a waterborne view, or by bicycle, available for rent from Capitol Bikeshare *(capitalbikeshare.com)*. To avoid peak crowds, try visiting the Tidal Basin early or late in the day.

National Cherry Blossom Festival

The National Cherry Blossom Festival *(national cherryblossomfestival.org)* has taken place since 1927, today drawing more than 1.5 million visitors with hundreds of mostly free events and activities offered over four weekends. Highlights include the parade on Constitution Avenue *(between 7th & 17th Sts., N.W.)*, with its elaborate floats, entertainers, and marching bands; the Sakura Matsuri–Japanese Street Festival on Pennsylvania Avenue *(between 9th & 14th Sts., N.W.)*; and the Blossom Kite Festival on the Washington Monument grounds.

BEYOND **THE TIDAL BASIN**

Here are some other beautiful, lesser known places for *hanami:*

East Potomac Park More cherry trees near the Tidal Basin, along the Potomac River and Washington Channel. *nps.gov*

Kenwood A Bethesda, Maryland, neighborhood that offers an excellent Plan B. *visitmontgomery.com*

U.S. National Arboretum Many different varieties of cherries, blooming at different times. *usna.usda.gov*

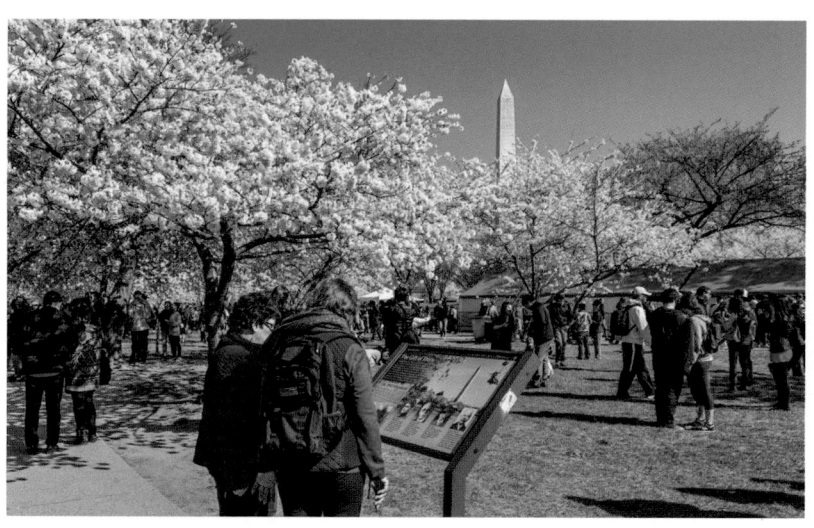

Free Entertainment

Washington is famous for its free admission to some of the world's greatest museums. A lesser known fact is that there are many free cultural events as well, especially throughout the summer. From big bands to big screens, cool jazz to contemporary theater, here are some of the best.

NATIONAL MALL

■ SUMMER MILITARY BAND CONCERTS

Get into the patriotic spirit with the music of talented U.S. military bands performing at outdoor concerts throughout the summer. Catch the **U.S. Navy Band** (*www.navyband.navy.mil*) at 8 p.m. Mondays at the U.S. Capitol or at 7:30 p.m. Tuesdays at the U.S. Navy Memorial. The **U.S. Air Force Band** (*www.usafband.af.mil*) plays at 8 p.m. Tuesdays at the U.S. Capitol; 8 p.m. Wednesdays at the National Sylvan Theater, in front of the Washington Monument; and 8 p.m. Fridays at the U.S. Air Force Memorial in Arlington. The **U.S. Marine Band** (*www.marineband.marines.mil*) plays at 8 p.m. Wednesdays at the U.S. Capitol. And finally, the rousing **U.S. Army Band** (*www.usarmyband.com*) performs before the U.S. Capitol on Fridays at 8 p.m. Additional concerts are listed on the respective websites.

■ A CAPITOL FOURTH

Washington offers many ways to celebrate the Fourth of July, including the televised "A Capitol Fourth" concert on the West Lawn of the U.S. Capitol building—an evening of music capped by fireworks over glowing monuments. It's all free, but people start lining up for entry well before the 8 p.m. start time.

National Mall • pbs.org/a-capitol-fourth • Metro: Smithsonian

■ JAZZ IN THE GARDEN

On sultry Friday evenings between Memorial Day and Labor Day, bebop to a wide variety of jazz amid giant sculptures at the National Gallery of Art's Sculpture Garden. Bands play between 5 p.m. and 8:30 p.m. Purchase food (and sangria!) from the Pavilion Café or bring your own picnic basket.

National Gallery of Art Sculpture Garden, Constitution Ave. & 7th St., N.W. • tel 202-289-3360 • nga.gov • Metro: Smithsonian

The U. S. Navy Band performs in front of the United States Capitol as part of the group's free summer evening concert series.

■ MILLENNIUM STAGE

Perhaps one of the greatest finds in Washington is the Kennedy Center's Millennium Stage, where local, national, and international artists present music, dance, and theater at 6 p.m. For free! You don't need a ticket, but seating is limited and available only on a first-come, first-served basis. Check the website to see who's performing next. You can also join a free guided tour.

John F. Kennedy Center for the Performing Arts, 2700 F St., N.W. • tel 202-467-4600 or 800-444-1324 • kennedy-center.org • Metro: Foggy Bottom–GWU

■ THE YARDS PARK AT CAPITOL RIVERFRONT

Enjoy live music on Friday evenings at the lovely waterfront setting of The Yards Park (see sidebar p. 72) along the Anacostia River, near Nationals Park baseball stadium. Spread a blanket on grassy open space and purchase a ready-made picnic at one of the nearby restaurants—or bring your own. Check the website to see which band is on tap—the variety ranges from reggae to country to indie.

The Yards Park, Capitol Riverfront, 35 Water St., S.E. • tel 202-465-7080 • yardspark.org • Metro: Navy Yard–Ballpark

CAPITOL HILL

Capitol Hill

The seat of the world's foremost democratic power rises on a swell of land on the National Mall's eastern edge—a site that civil planner Pierre-Charles L'Enfant described as a "pedestal waiting for a superstructure." Architect William Thornton designed the white-marble, Pantheon-like dome flanked by symmetrical wings of the Senate and the House, and George Washington himself laid the cornerstone in 1793. The Capitol remained the only government building on "the Hill" until the late 19th century, when it was joined by the Library of Congress's Jefferson Building, and Daniel H. Burnham's Union Station and Washington City Post Office. In the 1930s the U.S. Supreme Court, Folger Shakespeare Library, and more were added to the mix. The surrounding Capitol Hill neighborhood, with its historic row houses, is a lovely place to stroll, especially in springtime. Eastern Market comes alive on weekends with outdoor markets, while Barracks Row (Eighth Street) has blossomed with trendy restaurants and bars.

70 **Neighborhood Walk**

78 **In Depth:
U.S. Capitol**

82 **Distinctly D.C.:
Capital City**

84 **Best Of:
Watering Holes**

◀ **Representations
of past patriots and
heroes, chosen by
the individual states,
adorn the U.S. Capitol's
two-story National
Statuary Hall.**

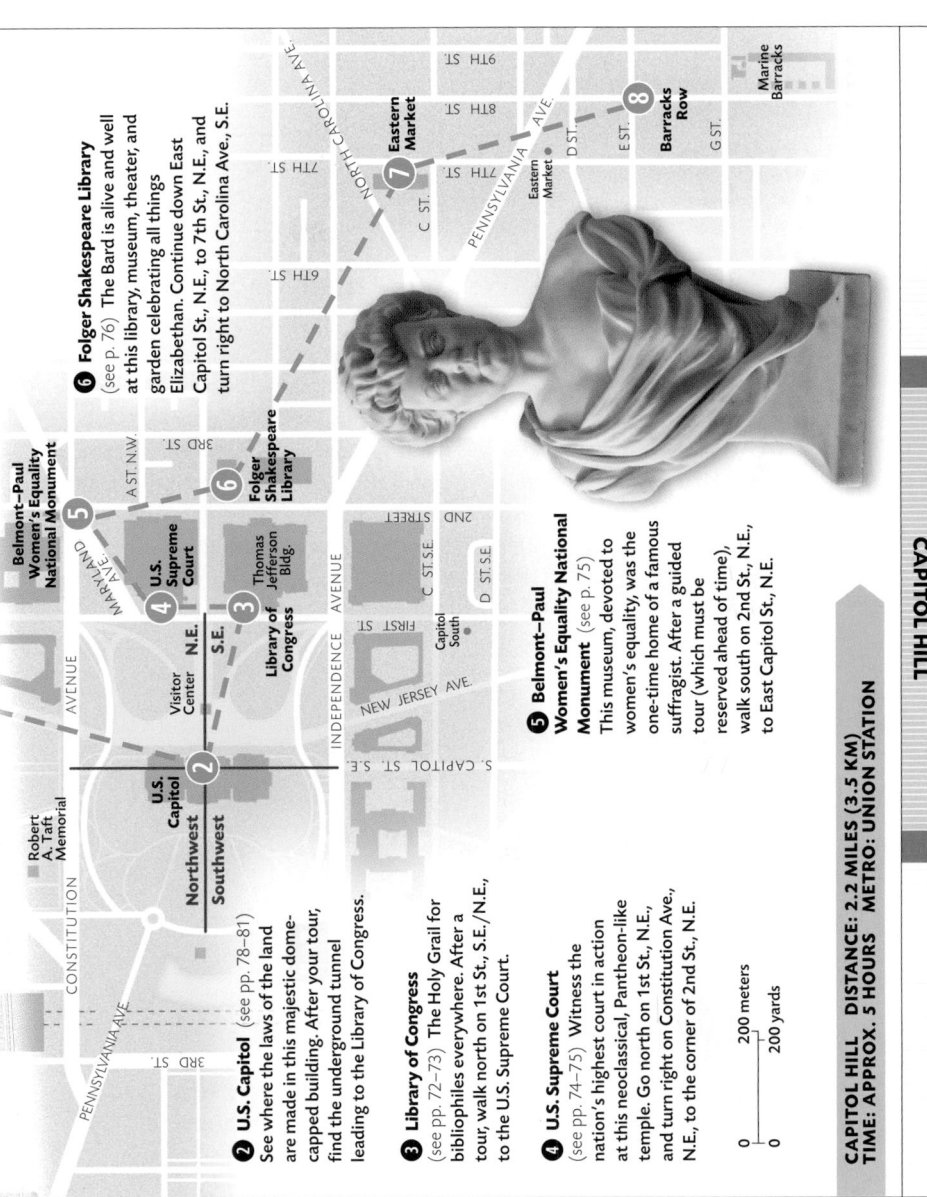

2 U.S. Capitol (see pp. 78–81) See where the laws of the land are made in this majestic dome-capped building. After your tour, find the underground tunnel leading to the Library of Congress.

3 Library of Congress (see pp. 72–73) The Holy Grail for bibliophiles everywhere. After a tour, walk north on 1st St., S.E./N.E., to the U.S. Supreme Court.

4 U.S. Supreme Court (see pp. 74–75) Witness the nation's highest court in action at this neoclassical, Pantheon-like temple. Go north on 1st St., N.E., and turn right on Constitution Ave., N.E., to the corner of 2nd St., N.E.

5 Belmont–Paul Women's Equality National Monument (see p. 75) This museum, devoted to women's equality, was the one-time home of a famous suffragist. After a guided tour (which must be reserved ahead of time), walk south on 2nd St., N.E., to East Capitol St., N.E.

6 Folger Shakespeare Library (see p. 76) The Bard is alive and well at this library, museum, theater, and garden celebrating all things Elizabethan. Continue down East Capitol St., N.E., to 7th St., N.E., and turn right to North Carolina Ave., S.E.

CAPITOL HILL DISTANCE: 2.2 MILES (3.5 KM)
TIME: APPROX. 5 HOURS   METRO: UNION STATION

0 — 200 meters
0 — 200 yards

CAPITOL HILL

Robert A. Taft Memorial

CONSTITUTION   AVENUE

PENNSYLVANIA AVE

3RD ST.

U.S. Capitol

Northwest
Southwest

S. CAPITOL ST., S.E.

Visitor Center

N.E.

S.E.

INDEPENDENCE   AVENUE

NEW JERSEY AVE.

FIRST ST.

Capitol South

Library of Congress

Thomas Jefferson Bldg.

2ND   STREET

C ST. S.E.

D ST. S.E.

U.S. Supreme Court

MARYLAND AVE.

Belmont–Paul Women's Equality National Monument

A ST. N.W.

3RD ST.

Folger Shakespeare Library

NORTH CAROLINA AVE.

7TH ST.

6TH ST.

C ST.

PENNSYLVANIA   AVE.

7TH ST.

Eastern Market

8TH ST.

9TH ST.

D ST.

E ST.

G ST.

Eastern Market

Barracks Row

Marine Barracks

IN **THE KNOW**

The Yards Park, a 15- to 20-minute walk away from the Hill, is the perfect place to relax. A revitalized stretch of land along the Anacostia River, it has a boardwalk, fountains, and a terraced lawn where bands play on summer Friday evenings (see p. 67). It's part of the larger Yards project, which offers restaurants and bars galore and—not too far away—Nationals Park, home of the MLB team the Washington Nationals. *yardspark.org*

Union Station

1 Start your day with coffee at this majestic train station, modeled in part after the Baths of Caracalla and Diocletian and the Arch of Rome—and definitely worth visiting just for its architecture. Grand arches give way to the triumphal, echoing **Main Hall,** where 36 larger-than-life Roman legionnaires preside on the gallery level. A barrel-vaulted ceiling with gold-leaf coffers soars above the station's bustle; more than 90,000 visitors pass through here every day, some stopping at the 100-plus specialty shops and restaurants. It's undergoing a major, 8.5-billion-dollar expansion and redevelopment plan, complete with a hotel and parks. The "Union Station Tour" app includes a self-guided tour and an interactive scavenger hunt.

2 West/40 Massachusetts Ave., N.E. • tel 202-289-1908 • unionstationdc.com • Metro: Union Station

U.S. Capitol

2 See pp. 78–81.

East Capitol St., N.E., & 1st St., S.E. • tel 202-226-8000 • visitthecapitol.gov • book tours through your Congressperson, online, or obtain first-come, first-served tickets at the visitor center • Metro: Capitol South

Library of Congress

3 Truly a glorious temple of learning, the Italian Renaissance–style Thomas Jefferson building of the Library of Congress—the main building—dazzles the eye with its opulent yet tasteful cornucopia of sculpture, mural mosaics, and architectural flourishes. The world's largest library, the Library of Congress has 160 million items, including President Washington's 1789 first inaugural address; the first map to name America, the Waldseemüller map; and 2,100 baseball cards dating from 1887 to 1914. You can take an organized

Allegorical statues representing civilization and learning, as well as great thinkers of the past, watch over today's scholars from the galleries of the Main Reading Room, Library of Congress.

CAPITOL HILL

tour of the Jefferson Building or pick up a self-guided tour brochure at the visitor center just inside the west side's ground level entrance. At the very least, don't miss the gilded **Great Hall** on the first floor, where you'll feel as if you've entered a Mediterranean palazzo. Nearby, two Library treasures rest behind glass cases: the Giant Bible of Mainz and the Gutenberg Bible, both made in Germany in the mid-1450s. Then climb the stairs to peer down into the historic **Main Reading Room,** whose 250 desks are arranged under a dome 160 feet (49 m) above the floor. With extra time, peruse the second floor's side galleries, featuring permanent and rotating exhibitions of American history and culture. Want a closer look at the Library's offerings? Use your driver's license or passport to obtain your own library card. Even if you don't use it, it makes for a great souvenir.

Thomas Jefferson Bldg., 10 1st St., S.E. • tel 202-707-8000 • loc.gov • Metro: Capitol South, Union Station

U.S. Supreme Court

4 In this imposing neoclassical building, the nation's highest tribunal hears cases involving the Constitution or the nation's laws. It's here that the nation's most famous and influential decisions have been handed down. From the front plaza, you enter on the ground floor, where **exhibitions** delve into the court's history and architecture—you'll see Chief Justice John Marshall's bench chair (used between 1819 and 1835), a calendar depicting the first month of action (October 1935), and models providing insight into the symbolism behind the East and West Pediments. Crane your neck up at the five-story, marble-and-bronze **spiral staircases,** designed by the building's architect, Cass Gilbert, and watch the introductory 24-minute film. Then climb the majestic stairs to the **Great Hall** on the first floor and its long line of busts depicting

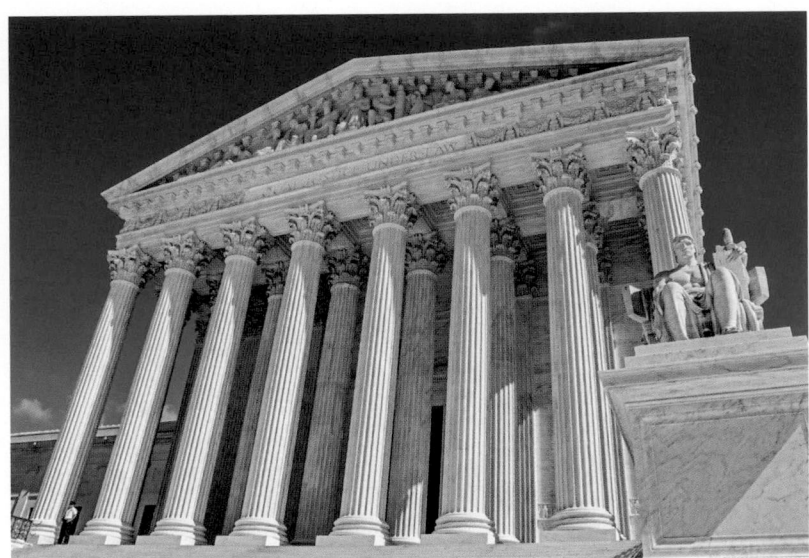

The U.S. Supreme Court's west facade proclaims the guiding principle, "Equal Justice Under Law."

former chief justices. At the end of the hall lies the actual **courtroom,** which you can look into when the court is not in session. Docents offer lectures here every hour on the half-hour, covering the judicial functions of the Supreme Court as well as the building's history and architecture. When the court is in session *(Oct.–mid-May)*, you can listen to oral arguments by lining up on the Front Plaza; the schedule is on the website. Note there is a line for those who just want to hear a three-minute sample of the case.

1st St., N.E. • tel 202-479-3000 • supremecourt.gov • closed Sat.–Sun. • Metro: Capitol South, Union Station

Belmont–Paul Women's Equality National Monument

5 Robert Sewall built this two-story brick house in 1799 and later rented it to Albert Gallatin, secretary of the treasury, from 1801 to 1813 (he probably penned the Louisiana Purchase here). But it's perhaps most famous for being the staging ground for feminist education and social change. Multimillionaire socialite and suffragist Alva Belmont helped purchase the house in 1929 for the National Women's Party, a nonpartisan organization that lobbied for women's rights for more than 60 years. Alice Stokes Paul, lifelong activist for women's equality and author of the proposed Equal Rights Amendment, was the house's primary resident for 40 years. The museum has recently been brought to greater prominence, after President Obama designated the house a national monument in 2016. Among the sepia photographs and fading banners, you'll also find personal items of two icons of the women's suffrage movement, Susan B. Anthony and Elizabeth Cady Stanton. Call ahead for a tour or reserve a spot online.

144 Constitution Ave., N.E. • tel 202-546-1210 • nps.gov/bepa, sewallbelmont.org • by guided tour only: Thurs.–Sat. • $$ • Metro: Capitol South, Union Station

GOOD **EATS**

■ **MR. HENRY'S RESTAURANT**
Serving the Hill since 1966, this hole-in-the-wall jazz joint serves creative pub grub. **601 Pennsylvania Ave., S.E., tel 202-546-8412, $$**

■ **MONTMARTRE**
A delightful French bistro with outdoor seating. **327 7th St., S.E., tel 202-544-1244, closed Mon., $$$**

■ **TED'S BULLETIN RESTAURANT**
Comfort food with a twist: peanut butter bacon burgers, grilled-cheese-and-tomato soup, and adult milkshakes. **505 8th St., S.E., tel 202-544-8337, $$**

CAPITOL HILL

Folger Shakespeare Library

6 This unique library, dedicated in 1932, holds the world's largest collection of William Shakespeare's printed works from the 16th century to present day, plus a world-famous collection of prints, manuscripts, and books. Before you enter, notice the marble, art deco–inspired, neoclassical exterior, adorned with nine bas-relief scenes from Shakespearean plays. Inside, you are greeted by Shakespeare's Tudor world, highlighted by the oak-paneled **Great Hall.** Changing exhibits in this large room showcase some of the library's vast collection, always focusing on some theme relevant to the life and times of Shakespeare, such as the role of women in medicine. Look in the hall's southeastern corner for the **Shakespeare First Folio,** the first collected edition of Shakespeare's plays and the only source for 18 of his plays—without which these dramatic treasures would have been lost forever. Through the door at the Great Hall's eastern end, you enter into the foyer leading to the **Folger Theatre,** a replication of the Elizabethan Globe Theatre. Feel free to walk around and take a look—though it's definitely worth returning in the evening to see the stage in action. Guided tours are available of the Tudor-style **Paster Reading Room** (pull aside the curtains from the Great Hall for a peek), complete with a 16th-century Jacobean table. The bust of Shakespeare on the east wall is one of two approved likenesses. Outside, an enchanting **Elizabethan flower and herb garden** is filled with plants popular during Shakespeare's lifetime; it can be seen only by guided tour from April through October.

201 E. Capitol St., S.E. • tel 202-544-4600 • folger.edu • see website for docent-led and special tour schedules • Metro: Union Station, South Capitol

Eastern Market

7 Since 1873, Eastern Market has been the residential heart of Capitol Hill, a draw for locals and visitors alike. Tuesday through Sunday, local merchants at the indoor **South Hall Market** purvey all the makings for a gourmet picnic: wonderful meats, seafood, cheese, produce, baked goods, and more. Or if you want

Leafy streets, outdoor dining, and a friendly atmosphere add to the appeal of the Capitol Hill neighborhood around Eastern Market.

CAPITOL HILL

something made on the spot, line up at the **Market Lunch** counter *(tel 202-547-8444)*. On weekends, there's a bustling outdoor farmer's market; an arts and crafts market and antique dealers add to the mix.

225 7th St., S.E. • tel 202-698-5253 • easternmarket-dc.org, marketlunchdc.com • closed Mon. • Metro: Eastern Market

Barracks Row (Eighth Street)

8 After a long day, Washingtonians in the know head to this lively culinary scene that has injected new life into the city's oldest commercial corridor. Its name derives from the nearby U.S. Marine Corps Barracks, which it has long served, along with the nearby Washington Navy Yard. **Cultural Tourism DC** *(culturaltourismdc.org)* offers a self-guided heritage walking tour of the neighborhood, clearly marked by 16 poster-size signs along the way. Otherwise, this is a great place to sip a cocktail, linger over creative cuisine, and plan your next move.

8th St. bet. D & I Sts., S.E. • tel 202-544-3188 • barracksrow.org • Metro: Eastern Market

CAPITOL HILL

U.S. Capitol

*The center of America's political power rises majestically
on a hill in neoclassical splendor.*

**The U.S. Capitol's dome-topped center building is flanked by two wings hosting the chambers
of Congress: the House of Representatives to the south and the Senate to the north.**

Visible from vantage points across Washington, the regal U.S. Capitol building
serves as a constant reminder of the nation's democratic foundation. For it
is here, in its hallowed halls, that Congress meets and the many voices of the
union are brought together to discuss and create the laws of the land. Designed
by Dr. William Thornton in 1793 and partially burned by the British during
the War of 1812, the Capitol was fully restored in 1863 and is crowned by the
19.5-foot-tall (6 m) bronze statue of "Freedom."

■ U.S. CAPITOL VISITOR CENTER

Begin at the underground U.S. Capitol Visitor Center, which serves as the gateway for all tours. Be sure to take some time to stroll through **Emancipation Hall** on the lower level, which offers insightful exhibits incorporating original documents and interactive videos—don't miss the 11-foot-high (3 m) cross section of the Capitol dome at one-twentieth its size, both inside and out. At your allocated tour time, line up as directed. The tour starts with a 13-minute film explaining the history and role of Congress.

■ ORIGINAL FRONT DOOR

Starting on the building's south side, you'll enter via the Capitol's original front door, dating from 1793. Just inside, in the **Senate Vestibule,** Corinthian columns topped with corncobs are among the Capitol's oldest artifacts.

■ OLD SUPREME COURT

The U.S. Supreme Court, which originally met only twice a year, convened in this room between 1810 and 1860. The Dred Scott case was one of the most notable decisions made here. Note the number of chairs available for spectators. In the fledgling city, watching a Supreme Court prosecution was a high form of entertainment—and a great way to get caught up on the news of the day.

■ CRYPT

The nation's forefathers hoped that George and Martha Washington would be buried in the Capitol building, and a special place was designed for their final resting place. But they had other plans—they preferred to be laid to rest at their home in Mount Vernon. Today, the tomb remains empty, and the crypt now contains some of the **National Statuary Hall Collection**—you'll find the first 13 Colonies represented here. The beautiful sandstone columns were carved by enslaved people, as was much of the original Capitol building.

■ ROTUNDA

A trip up the stairs leads to the large and grandiose Rotunda. This glorious domed room is where Congress comes to celebrate—whether it's both sides of Congress convening to toast a new bill, receiving an esteemed visitor or head of state, or honoring an outstanding American upon their death. Only 33 people have lain in state here since the 1850s, including Rosa Parks (the only woman), Ronald Reagan, Abraham Lincoln, and John F. Kennedy. On the walls, four giant panels by John

SAVVY **TRAVELER**

Be advised that passes are required to tour the Capitol building. Book in advance online *(visitthecapitol.gov)*, through the offices of your senators or representative, or through the **Office of Visitor Services** *(tel 202/226-8000)*. A limited number of same-day passes are issued from the visitor center's lower level. Separate gallery passes are required to watch the House or Senate in session— you can request these in advance or in person from your senator or representative; international visitors should stop by the Appointments Desk at the visitor center. In addition, some congressional offices offer staff-led tours to constituent groups of up to 15 people, or they can help you book a general tour. If you just want to view the visitor center exhibits or have lunch at the restaurant, passes are not required. Note that drinks, food, and aerosol containers are not allowed in the Capitol building. Check the website for additional details as well as policies on etiquette and security.

Trumbull depict the American Revolution; with four other panels by various artists illustrating the themes of exploration and settlement (including Pocahontas's baptism before her marriage to John Rolfe). Be sure to look up at the dome's ceiling, where a fresco entitled "The Apotheosis of Washington," painted in 1865 by the Italian–American artist Constantino Brumidi, shows a dreamy, cloud-filled scene where George Washington is joined by 13 women symbolizing the 13 Colonies and American democracy. Among the many state statues in this room is one donated by Congress honoring the National Women's Party depicting Susan B. Anthony, Elizabeth Stanton, and Lucretia Mott—and there's room for one more woman because, as the sculptor believes, the story is still ongoing.

■ NATIONAL STATUARY HALL
This beautiful Greek Revival hall— one of the earliest examples in America—served as the House of Representatives between 1807 and 1857. Bronze plaques mark the spots where various representatives sat, including Abraham Lincoln and John Quincy Adams. Alas, the smooth, curved ceiling created poor acoustics, making it nearly impossible to understand debates as well as creating some "whispering spots," such as at Adams's desk, where you may clearly hear a soft voice from many yards away. The House moved to its present chamber in the House wing in 1857, and this room became the official National Statuary Hall. Beginning in 1864, every state was invited to send two statues to be displayed here—the only rules

"The Apotheosis of Washington" appears shrouded in clouds during a recent renovation.

being that the person must be dead, and the statue had to be marble or bronze. Today, one-third of Congress's collection of statues is found here, including ones of **Father Junípero Serra** (California), **Henry Clay** (Kentucky), and **Robert E. Lee** (Virginia).

■ GALLERIES

A separate pass is required to visit the Galleries (see sidebar opposite), where you can look down on either the House or Senate floors and view for yourself the long and complicated process of lawmaking.

■ U.S. CAPITOL GROUNDS

The Capitol sits on 58.8 acres (24 ha) of landscaped grounds designed by renowned landscape architect Frederick Law Olmsted. Take a stroll to enjoy the building from all angles, then follow pathways from its south side, down the hill to the **U.S. Botanic Garden** (see p. 156). Cross in front of the **Capitol Reflecting Pool,** taking note of the statue of General Grant (the nation's largest equestrian statue), before climbing up the other side. You'll come across pocket gardens, memorial trees, hidden statues, and plenty of benches.

East Capitol St., N.E., *&* 1st St., S.E. • tel 202-226-8000 • visitthecapitol.gov • Metro: Capitol South

Capital City

Washington, D.C., was founded in 1790 to serve exclusively as the fledgling nation's capital, where the president would live and where the laws of the land would be made and upheld. Topped by the majestic Capitol building and dotted with various congressional offices, much of Capitol Hill is devoted to making legislation. But its reach extends far beyond.

Above: This 1922 photograph shows how Washington's boundary stones—marking the perimeter of the District of Columbia—have long been worthy reminders of the Founding Fathers' ideas for the nation's capital. Opposite: A stylized "View of Washington City" circa 1852. A larger Capitol dome was completed in 1866.

Why Washington?

Alexander Hamilton wanted the new government to be located in the North. Thomas Jefferson wanted the capital within reach of the agricultural South. George Washington made the final decision—a 100-square-mile (259 sq km) area carved out of Maryland and Virginia near his home at Mount Vernon. The compromise offered an accessible trade route to the western frontier via the Potomac and Ohio River Valleys.

L'Enfant Hired

The city's original plan was devised by Frenchman Pierre-Charles L'Enfant, who came to America to fight the Revolutionary War. He ended up designing the Capital City on what was, essentially, a clean slate of undulating, plantation-dotted landscape. Using European models with a dash of American ideals, he placed Congress on the highest point (where in Europe the leader's house would be) with wide avenues radiating beyond, punctuated by important buildings and attractive squares and parks. Centerpiece of it all: The 400-foot-wide (122 m), tree-lined "grand avenue" that later became the National Mall.

L'Enfant Fired

But L'Enfant's perfectionist traits led to his being fired. Eventually the city's surveyor, Andrew Ellicott, took over with a plan based on L'Enfant's vision, but with the compromises he refused to consider (the waterfall cascading off Capitol Hill, for example, was scratched). However, the capital remained incomplete for more than a century; even after the Civil War there was talk of moving the capital to Philadelphia or the Midwest.

At Long Last

The McMillan Commission was formed in 1902, taking to task the completion of the Capital City. Still within the confines of L'Enfant's original plan, they built parks and reclaimed land to make space for the Lincoln and Jefferson Memorials. At long last, elegant Washington began to emerge, an impression that remains to this day.

BOUNDARY **STONES**

When the original perimeter of Washington, D.C., was surveyed, the 10-by-10-mile (16 x 16 km) outline was marked with sandstone cairns one mile (1.6 km) apart—supervised by George Washington himself. The nation's oldest federal monuments, 36 of the 40 stones remain in place to this day. They are a popular treasure hunt for walkers and bikers, and a great way to delve into D.C.'s varied neighborhoods. Some are obvious, others not so. That's what makes a boundary-stone quest so fun!
boundarystones.org

Watering Holes

Washington has a long tradition of watering holes frequented by politicians and everyone else in need of a place to unwind after work, discuss a deal, and talk the talk. And, as every Hill intern knows, many bars offer well-priced happy hours, complete with free or inexpensive snacks.

■ THE MONOCLE

The location as the closest eatery to the Senate side of the Capitol virtually guarantees politico-sightings. (Hint: Look for the lapel button worn by members of Congress.) It opened in 1960, when regular customers Richard M. Nixon and John F. Kennedy were battling for the presidency. Autographed photographs hanging on the walls span decades of Hill history. It's a restaurant, too, serving an all-American menu of burgers, steaks, and seafood.

107 D St., N.E. • tel 202-546-4488
• themonocle.com • Metro: Union Station

■ HAWK 'N' DOVE

Established in 1967, this longtime Capitol Hill favorite attracts locals, congressional staffers, and the occasional political celebrity. A relatively recent renovation has done away with the warren of hidden rooms, opening up the space with a contemporary look. Burgers, sandwiches, and beer dominate the menu.

329 Pennsylvania Ave., S.E. • tel 202-547-0030
• hawkndovebardc.com • Metro: Capitol South

■ POV

You don't get much better views than from the rooftop balcony of the W hotel's POV (point of view) bar—a bird's-eye angle of the White House to one side, the monument-dotted Mall on the other. On a clear day, if you squint to the west, you can just make out the eternal flame flickering off in Arlington National Cemetery, beyond the Lincoln Memorial. Owned by W Hotels and Resorts, the former Hotel Washington offers cushioned sofas, lounge chairs, and an imaginative drinks menu. The only downside: the long lines of crowds waiting to get in.

W Washington D.C. , 515 15th St., N.W.
• tel 202-661-2400 • wwashingtondc.com
• Metro: Metro Center

Where deals go down: The back bar at Old Ebbitt Grill, site of many political assignations

■ OLD EBBITT GRILL

A favorite haunt of former Presidents Ulysses S. Grant, Grover Cleveland, and Theodore Roosevelt, this D.C. staple was founded in 1856 and is Washington's oldest, most historic saloon (though the current building dates from 1983). It remains a popular spot for D.C. celebrities, journalists, and politicians. Always crowded, the large restaurant offers a menu full of burgers, grilled fish, and a notable selection of oysters. The walrus head hanging in the bar is reputed to have been bagged by Theodore Roosevelt.

675 15th St., N.W. • tel 202-347-4800 • ebbitt.com • Metro: Metro Center

■ ROUND ROBIN BAR

The bar of choice for presidential discussions—whether you're a president-elect, politician, lobbyist, reporter, or general onlooker—ever since it opened in the Willard hotel in 1850. Mark Twain and Walt Whitman are among those who have lingered here through the years. The bartender, Jim Hewes, is nearly as famous as the hotel; he's been tending bar here for more than 30 years. The adjacent Scotch Bar is also popular.

Willard InterContinental Washington, 1401 Pennsylvania Ave., N.W. • tel 202-628-9100 • washington.intercontinental.com • Metro: Metro Center

DOWNTOWN

N.W. N.E.

S.E.

Potomac

Downtown

Just north of Pennsylvania Avenue, N.W., between 14th and 7th Streets, and reaching as far north as Louisiana and Massachusetts Avenues, N.W., Washington's downtown area booms with the bustle of everyday urban life. This corner of the city suffered great devastation during the 1968 riots after the assassination of Martin Luther King, Jr. In the following years, area crime skyrocketed as buildings fell into decay. But downtown is looking up: Revitalization has come to stay, kick-started with the arrival of the MCI Center (now Capitol One Arena) sports and events complex in 1997— home to the Washington Wizards NBA basketball team and Washington Capitals NHL team, as well as world-class entertainment events. Here, in a vibrant area dubbed Penn Quarter, über-trendy restaurants, boutiques, art galleries, and theaters thrive. Amid all this buzz, don't overlook several excellent museums, including the Smithsonian American Art Museum and National Portrait Gallery, and the ever popular International Spy Museum.

88 **Neighborhood Walk**

96 **In Depth: Smithsonian American Art Museum and National Portrait Gallery**

100 **Distinctly D.C.: Theater Scene**

102 **Best Of: Small Museums**

◀ **Four tiers of arcades face two sets of huge columns within the light-filled Great Hall of the National Building Museum, built to resemble a vast Italian palazzo.**

Downtown

Located in the Northwest quadrant, to the north of the National Mall and the broad swath of Pennsylvania Avenue, Washington's vibrant downtown area booms with restaurants, shops, theaters, and galleries.

❶ Freedom Plaza (see p. 90)
Look down to see the inlaid bronze map depicting L'Enfant's original city plan on this granite plaza. Then set your sights on the Capitol as you walk down Pennsylvania Ave., N.W., to 9th St., N.W. turn right on 9th St. and then left on Constitution Ave.

❷ National Archives
(see pp. 90–91) Pay your respects to the nation's most important documents—the Constitution and Declaration of Independence among them. Return to 8th St., N.W., and walk north to E St., N.W.; turn left.

❸ J. Edgar Hoover FBI Building
(see pp. 91–92) Take the "FBI Experience" self-guided tour to learn how detectives gumshoe crime and espionage. Continue on E Ave., N.W.; turn right on 10th St., N.W.

DOWNTOWN   DISTANCE: 2.2 MILES (3.5 KM)
TIME: APPROX. 12 HOURS   METRO: FEDERAL TRIANGLE, METRO CENTER

❻ National Building Museum
(see p. 94) An imposing building with fascinating exhibits related to architecture. Cross F St., walk across Judiciary Sq. Walk west on E St. and turn left on 6th St.

❼ Woolly Mammoth Theatre
(see p. 95) Live an edgy theater experience. Walk north on 6th St. and turn right on E St.

❽ National Law Enforcement Memorial and Museum (see pp. 94–95) Learn what it's like to be a cop and test your knowledge and skills in D.C.'s newest interactive museum.

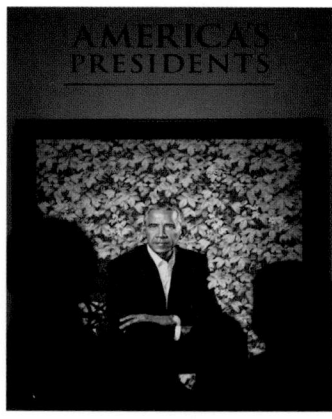

AMERICA'S PRESIDENTS

❺ Smithsonian American Art Museum and National Portrait Gallery
(see pp. 96–99) Albert Bierstadt, Mary Cassatt, and John La Farge are among the American artists applauded in this bright, beautifully curated art museum paired with a portrait gallery notable for its lineup of U.S. presidents. Continue east on F St., N.W.

❹ Ford's Theatre N.H.S. (see p. 93)
Visit the still active theater where Lincoln was killed, as well as its insightful museum. Continue up 10th St., N.W., to F St., N.W., and turn right for 1.5 blocks.

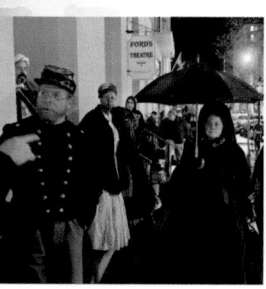

Freedom Plaza

1 This modernist granite plaza, built in 1980 and overlooked by an equestrian statue of Polish military commander Casimir Pulaski, includes an inlaid map of L'Enfant's original plan for the city. Renamed in honor of Martin Luther King, Jr., who wrote much of his "I Have a Dream" speech nearby, its grand, sweeping view down Pennsylvania Avenue all the way to the Capitol makes a telegenic backdrop to the various political protests that often convene here.

Pennsylvania Ave., bet. 13th & 14th Sts., N.W. • tel 202-619-7222 • nps.gov
• Metro: Federal Triangle, Metro Center

National Archives

2 The Charters of Freedom—the **Declaration of Independence, Constitution,** and **Bill of Rights**—are the star attractions in this grand neoclassical edifice, designed in 1935 for the express purpose of housing America's most revered documents. More than 12 billion paper records dating back to 1774 are preserved here (and billions more recent electronic records as well), though most are kept behind the scenes. Enter from Constitution Avenue, where the interactive **"Records of Rights"** exhibit addresses how the ideals enshrined in the original Charters of Freedom did not initially apply to all Americans—African Americans, women, Native Americans, and immigrants among them. Upstairs, in the hushed silence of the **Rotunda,** the Charters of Freedom are displayed in state-of-the-art cases. New York artist Barry Faulkner painted the two large murals hanging above the documents: "The Constitution" on the right, with George Washington in his white cape the obvious centerpiece; and "The Declaration of Independence" on the left (the figures for both are identified in nearby charts). On this floor, too, the fascinating and enormous **"Public Vaults"** exhibit delves deeply into the stacks, with videos, photographs, maps, and interpretive panels on display,

DOWNTOWN

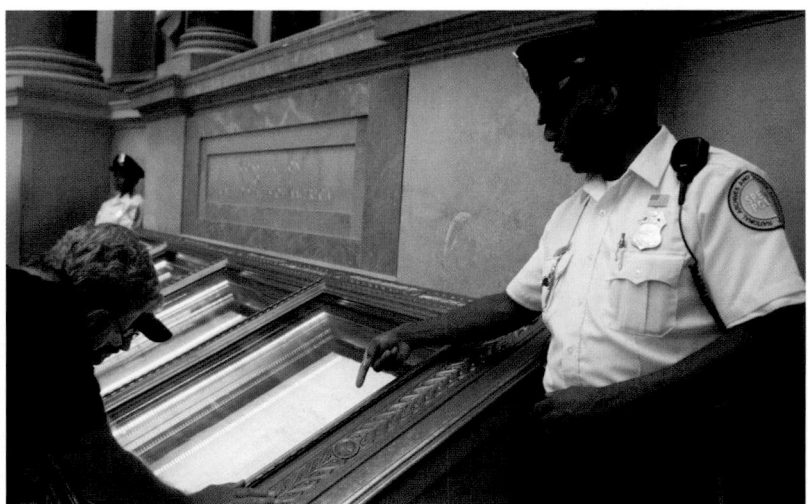

The nation's Charters of Freedom are fiercely guarded at the National Archives in specially designed aluminum and titanium cases, with the documents surrounded by an inert gas.

DOWNTOWN

as well as some of the archives' more interesting documents—from George Washington's handwritten letters to Abraham Lincoln's wartime telegrams to original D-Day footage.

Constitution Ave. bet. 7th & 9th Sts., N.W. • tel 866-272-6272 • archives.gov • Metro: Archives–Navy Memorial–Penn Quarter

J. Edgar Hoover FBI Building

3 Bounded by Pennsylvania Ave. and E St., and 9th and 10th Sts., the "Brutalist" FBI building of poured concrete contrasts sharply with the elegant neoclassical granite and marble government buildings around it. Completed in 1974 as the Federal Bureau of Investigation headquarters, its 2,800,876 sq ft (260,210 sq m) house more than 7,000 FBI agents and other employees. Although the building is otherwise off-limits, the Education Center offers a fascinating self-guided tour—"The FBI Experience"—that teaches about the agency's role in protecting the nation. Check out the desk of J. Edgar Hoover, the infamous FBI Director for whom the building is named; and the case with ephemera from the World Trade Center debris following the terrorist attacks of 9/11. And try to spot the surveillance camera hidden in a painting. Hint: Look closely at the period in the artist's signature). You can even watch FBI agents blasting away on the firing range! Note the ten American flags flying from the façade on Pennsylvania Ave: Each is different, with the earliest being the "Continental Colors" first raised on January 1, 1776. All visitors must be U.S. citizens or permanent residents, and visits must be scheduled through your congressional representative's office no later than four weeks in advance.

Corner E St., N.W. & 9th St., N.W. • fbi.gov •closed Sat. & Sun • Metro: Federal Triangle, Gallery Place-Chinatown, Archives-Navy Memorial-Penn Quarter

The Friendship Arch stands at the entrance to D.C.'s Chinatown, established in the 1930s.

Ford's Theatre National Historic Site

4 History was forever changed on the evening of April 14, 1865, when John Wilkes Booth shot President Abraham Lincoln in the Presidential Box of this theater, five days after Lee's surrender at Appomattox. The theater remained closed for more than a hundred years; the National Park Service acquired it in 1933, restored it to its original 1865 splendor in the 1960s, and renovated it once again in 2009. Today's visitors enter the museum downstairs, among absorbing exhibits exploring Lincoln's life. Look for such noteworthy artifacts as the .44-caliber derringer pistol Booth used in the shooting, Booth's escape diary, and the frock coat Lincoln was wearing on that fateful evening. Then climb the stairs to the Dress Circle and Balcony, overlooking the stage and the flag-draped **Presidential Box,** which has been authentically re-created with red velvet wallpaper, plush seats, and the original settee. In addition to the Park Service tours, the theater hosts a full program of contemporary American plays.

Continue your tour across the street to the **Petersen House,** where Lincoln was frantically carried as his life slipped away. Peek into the parlor where Mary Todd Lincoln nervously paced through the night; the back parlor where Edwin Stanton, Lincoln's secretary of war, began investigating the murder; and the bedroom where Lincoln died. From here, an elevator whisks you to more exhibits on three separate floors, describing Lincoln's world. Timed tickets are free, but reservations are required; visit the website for additional information.

511 10th St., N.W. • tel 202-347-4833 • nps.gov/foth or fords.org • Metro: Federal Triangle, Gallery Place-Chinatown, Archives-Navy Memorial- Penn Quarter

IN **THE KNOW**

Only a few vestiges remain of Washington's original Chinese neighborhood; most of it has long been subsumed by Penn Quarter, with small remnants found in Chinese-written street signs, the colorful **Friendship Arch** on H Street, and the annual Chinese New Year Parade. If you find yourself craving Chinese cuisine among the wide selection of ethnic cuisines on offer here, dig your chopsticks into some chow foon at **China Boy** *(817 6th St., N.W.)* or **Chinatown Express** *(746 6th St., N.W.).*

DOWNTOWN

DOWNTOWN

Life masks of Abraham Lincoln from 1860 (left) and 1865 (center) convey the toll of the Civil War.

Smithsonian American Art Museum and National Portrait Gallery

5 800 G St., N.W. ; enter via F St., N.W. • tel 202-633-1000
• americanart.si.edu, npg.si.edu • Metro: Gallery Place–Chinatown

National Building Museum

6 This monumental, redbrick 1887 building, modeled after Rome's 16th-century Palazzo Farnese for the U.S. Pension Bureau headquarters, is now a fascinating museum devoted to architecture, urban planning, and design. In the airy **Great Hall**— as large as an American football field—enormous Corinthian columns tower 75 feet (23 m). The Great Hall's first two levels offer innovative changing exhibits; permanent collections include an exploration of what it means to live at home in America. Several rooms allow hands-on building for kids.

401 F St., N.W. • tel 202-272-2448 • nbm.org • closed Mon. • exhibitions: $$ • Metro: Judiciary Square, Gallery Place–Chinatown

Woolly Mammoth Theatre

7 After dinner at one of Penn Quarter's many buzzing restaurants, head to the theater. Edgy and outside-the-box Woolly Mammoth produces quirky, fun, original works that you would be hard-pressed to find anywhere else. Or try the acclaimed **Shakespeare Theatre Company at the Harman Center for the Arts** in two Penn Quarter locations *(Sidney Harman Hall, 610 F St., N.W., and Lansburgh Theatre, 450 7th St., N.W., tel 202-547-1122, shakespearetheatre.org).*

Or catch a game or concert at the 20,000-seat **Capitol One Arena** (*601 F St., N.W., tel 202-628-3200, capitalonearena.viewlift. com*).

641 D St., N.W. • tel 202-393-3939 • woollymammoth.net • Metro: Archives–
Navy Memorial–Penn Quarter, Gallery Place–Chinatown

National Law Enforcement Memorial and Museum

8 Twin entrance pavilions fronting the D.C. Court of Appeals provide access to this underground museum extending beneath Judiciary Square, with its national monument to law enforcement officers. A plaque inset in the center of the square is cusped by 304-foot-long (92.5-m-long) blue-gray marble walls engraved with the names of more than 21,000 officers who have died in the line of duty since 1786. New names are added each May during National Police Week. Belowground, the museum displays an arresting assemblage of more than 20,000 artifacts, from a Colt M1849 Revolver issued to the Baltimore, MD, Police Department in 1857, and Al Capone's bulletproof vest, to the U.S. Park Police Eagle One helicopter used to rescue airplane crash survivors from the Potomac River on January 13, 1982. The museum's interactive exhibitions provide a captivating "walk in their shoes" immersive experience of American law enforcement. Be a 911 telephone operator in the interactive 9-1-1 Emergency Ops Dispatch Experience. Learn the forensic techniques that detectives use to solve crimes. And, gun in hand, hone your split-second decision making in the video Training Simulator.

444 E St., N.W. • tel 202-737-3400 • lawenforcementmu
seum.org • $$$$$ • Metro: Judiciary Square

DOWNTOWN

GOOD **EATS**

■ **JALEO**
Tapas in a festive setting, with good vegetarian options. **480 7th St., N.W., tel 202-628-7949, $$$**

■ **CLYDE'S OF GALLERY PLACE**
Classic American dishes with a buzzing ambiance. **707 7th St., N.W., tel 202-349-3700, $$**

■ **CITY TAP KITCHEN & CRAFT**
An American-style beer-focused brasserie famous for its burgers and pizzas. **901 9th St., N.W., tel 202-753-5333, $–$$$**

Smithsonian American Art Museum and National Portrait Gallery

The combined Smithsonian American Art Museum / National Portrait Gallery is one of North America's pre-eminent art collections.

Iconic images of heroism and horror form a special gallery of Pulitzer Prize winners.

These separate yet closely-related museums occupy the old U.S. Patent Building, a National Historic Landmark modeled on the Pantheon and considered one of the most grandiose neoclassical buildings in Washington. Taking up two city blocks in downtown's revitalized arts district, the twin museums share a main entrance on F Street and are known collectively as the Donald W. Reynolds Center for American Art and Portraiture. Covering an entire spectrum of American art spanning four centuries, you could spend an entire day here!

Smithsonian American Art Museum

SAAM houses a vast and all-encompassing collection of American art, displayed in themed galleries on three levels. Docent-led "Collection Highlights" tours are offered daily at 12:30 p.m. and 2 p.m.

■ Level One

Turn left in the entrance lobby to begin with **Experience America,** which includes art commissioned by the Works Progress Administration during the Depression, and the **Folk Art** gallery of works by self-taught and vernacular artists. Don't miss James Hampton's religiously-inspired "The Throne of the Third Heaven of the Nations' Millennium General Assembly", a complex 14-year labor fusing neighborhood detritus to evoke spiritual splendor and awe.

■ Level Two

Level Two's centuries-spanning collection charts the nation's growth from a young republic to a world power. Chronological and genre-themed galleries traverse **The American Colonies, The Early Republic, Antebellum Art** and **Civil War** to the **Gilded Age,** plus themes from **Southwestern Art to Modernism.** America's geographic wonders and westward expansion are

SAVVY **TRAVELER**

The Luce Foundation Center, on SAAM's third and fourth floors, offers informal sketching workshops every Tuesday at 2:30 p.m. So, bring a pad and pencil and your imagination and cater to your artistic muse as instructors teach you how to sketch works of art, from anatomy and portraits to landscapes.

extolled in such works as Albert Bierstadt's "Gates of the Yosemite"; while the museum's astounding "Indians Gallery" collection catalogs the lifeways and transformation of Native American cultures. Next, pass into the **Impressionist** gallery, displaying works by such late 19th-century masters as Childe Hassam and William Merritt Chase. You then enter the Gilded Age gallery, showing works by such hallmark early-20th-century painters as Winslow Homer, John Singer Sargent, and James McNeill Whistler; look for Homer's "High Cliff, Coast of Maine". Rounding out this floor are galleries dedicated to Southwestern Art and Modernism. The latter gallery ticks off works by a Who's Who of top American artists: Georgia O'Keeffe, John Sloan, Andrew Wyeth, and on and on. A highlight, Edward Hopper's "Cape Cod Morning" is an ode to postwar anxiety.

DOWNTOWN

■ LEVEL THREE

The museum has recently expanded its collection of late twentieth century and present-day works, displayed on this floor. SAAM's largest gallery combines sections dedicated to **Art Since 1945** and **Contemporary Art,** including cutting-edge video art and digital animation, such as Chris Burden's provocative early 1970s "performance pieces" reflecting the jarring social upheavals of the times. Look, too, for Roy Lichtenstein's "pop-art" pieces, and David Hockney's "Snails Space with Vari-Lites, 'Painting as Performance',". Scattered throughout the gallery are important examples of art by America's ethnic minorities, including photographs,

prints, sculpture, textiles, and paintings. And the comprehensive sculpture collection is highlighted by Deborah Butterfield's monumental horse, "Monekana", cast in bronze but appearing as if made of driftwood. The Mezzanine hosts the **Lunder Conservation Center,** where you can watch conservators at work in their sealed laboratories.

NATIONAL PORTRAIT GALLERY

Sharing each of the building's three levels, the **National Portrait** Gallery displays paintings, photographs, and sculptures of individuals who have come to define the United States as we know it, including portraits of every U.S. president and in all media, from daguerreotypes to digital.

■ LEVEL ONE

Start on the Portrait Gallery's first floor, with its **American Origins** exhibit of portraits arranged chronologically, starting with pre-Revolutionary War settlers and such Native Americans as Pocahontas dressed in Elizabethan garb. Three of the collection's 17 rooms are dedicated to Matthew Brady's Civil War–era collodion photography.

■ LEVEL TWO

After you climb the grand staircase to the second floor, turn to the right for

IN **THE KNOW**

The Robert and Arlene Kogod Courtyard, with its stunning wave-form glass-and-steel canopy, provides a contemporary counterpoint to the museums' Greek Revival architectural setting. Enclosing the former open-air atrium patio, the undulating canopy appears to float over the light-filled sanctuary, with its black granite floor. Designed by London's world-renowned Foster + Partners architects, the mesmerizing 28,000-square-foot (2,600 sq m) ceiling is supported by eight anodized aluminum-clad columns tucked against the courtyard perimeter. The overall effect elicits wonder and "Wows!" You can snack at the Courtyard Café while enjoying free musical performances and other public programs.

DOWNTOWN

American Presidents—the museum's centerpiece draw. Arranged in chronological order, this complete collection of U.S. presidents ranges from staged to fun. Highlights include Gilbert Stuart's famous "Lansdowne" 1796 portrait of George Washington; George P. A. Healy's pensive Abraham Lincoln; and Grover Cleveland's portrait, by Anders Leonard Zorn, in French Impressionist style. Bill Clinton's portrait by Chuck Close is a series of abstract modules that combine to give him a digital look. The museum's most popular portraits are those of President Barack Obama (by Kehinde Wiley) and Michelle Obama (by Amy Sherald); unveiled in February 2018, they became instant icons. This floor also hosts a revolving set of special exhibits, plus **The Struggle for Justice,** dedicated to Americans who have fought for civil rights equality throughout the years.

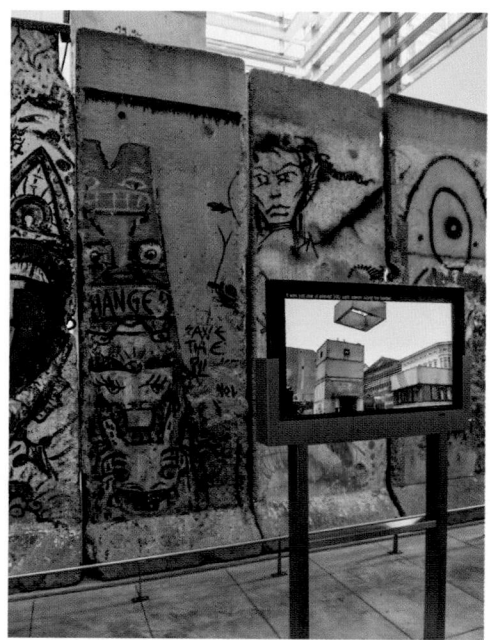

Video of the dismantling and a portion of the Berlin Wall put you on the front line of the Cold War.

■ LEVEL THREE

The grand staircase leads to yet another floor with galleries —**20th-Century Americans**—given to portraits of film stars, scientists, sports personalities, and statesmen covering the 1950s to the 1990s, from Arthur Ashe to John Wayne.

800 G St., N.W.; enter via F St., N.W. • tel 202-633-1000 • americanart.si.edu, npg.si.edu • Metro: Gallery Place–Chinatown

Theater Scene

Theatrical antics may prevail on Capitol Hill, but that shouldn't take away from the fact that Washington boasts one of the country's most thriving theater scenes, especially when it comes to experiential theater. Indeed, the numbers speak for themselves: 80-plus professional area theaters, more than 350 productions that run for more than 8,000 performances, more than 2 million audience members. When all is said and done, Washington is second only to New York in terms of the number of theater seats. And it's growing every year.

Above: Warner Theatre entrance in Downtown. Opposite: The historic Ford's Theatre, the site of President Lincoln's assassination, continues to host theater productions today.

In the Beginning

The ornate **National Theatre**—called the "Theater of Presidents" for its proximity to the White House—opened its doors in 1835 (in a different building on the same spot), making it the country's third-oldest theater. **Ford's Theatre** opened in 1862 as Ford's Athenaeum and presented a mix of comedies, variety shows, and Shakespearean plays. Alas, it's most famous for being the venue of President Abraham Lincoln's assassination. Dozens of theaters lit up downtown D.C. in the early 20th century, with "polite" or "high-class" vaudeville for middle class audiences. These included the **Warner Theatre,** originally opened as the Earle Theatre in 1924; today it's a major host of Broadway shows, dance, film, and music concerts.

Regional Theater

Founded in 1950, **Arena Stage** was one of the nation's first not-for-profit theaters, dedicated to focusing on the "canvas of American theater," including classics and new works. Washington boasts several other lauded regional theaters, including the **Shakespeare Theatre Company,** and the **Signature Theatre** in Arlington, Virginia.

Neighborhood Revival

Washington's theater scene changed dramatically about 20 years ago, when the D.C. government smartly offered grants to convert empty buildings in struggling neighborhoods into artistic venues. Directors and producers jumped at the chance. Thus was born a whole slew of new small theaters, where experimental and risky tactics are tried out and innovation is favored—Woolly Mammoth, Studio Theatre, and Theater J among them. See what's on stage via *dctheatrescene.com* and *culturecapital.com;* discounted tickets are available at *Goldstar.com.*

SMALL **THEATERS**

Regional theaters currently pushing the envelope include:

Atlas Performing Arts Center, 1333 H St., N.E., tel 202-399-7993, *atlasarts.org*

Signature Theatre, 4200 Campbell Ave., Arlington, VA, tel 703-820-9771, *sigtheatre.org*

Washington Improv Theater, 1835 14th St., N.W., 202-204-7770, *witdc.org*

Studio Theatre, 1501 14th St., N.W., tel 202-332-3300, *studiotheatre.org*

Theater J, 1529 16th St., N.W., tel 202-777-3210, *theaterj.org*

Woolly Mammoth Theatre Company, 641 D St., N.W., 202-393-3939, *woollymammoth.net*

DOWNTOWN

Small Museums

The National Mall's world-class museums may get all the attention, but Washington contains plenty of smaller museums that deserve a nod as well. The world's foremost museum devoted to women artists, a German brewer's Gilded Age manse, and a presidential summer cottage are among these hidden gems.

DOWNTOWN

■ NATIONAL MUSEUM
OF WOMEN IN THE ARTS
Showcasing more than 4,500 paintings and sculptures by more than 1,000 women artists, with work spanning from the 16th century to modern day, this lovely little museum founded in 1987 counts among its holdings stunning artwork by Frida Kahlo, Mary Cassatt, and Georgia O'Keeffe—indeed, it's considered the world's foremost collection of women's art. But it also celebrates talented women who didn't necessarily claim the fame they deserved. For examples, look for Lavinia Fontana's "Portrait of a Noblewoman" (ca 1580), Rosa Bonheur's "Highland Raid" (1860), and Justine Kurland's "Waterfall Mama Babies" (2006). The museum occupies a former Masonic Temple, built in glorious Renaissance Revival style.

1250 New York Ave., N.W. • tel 202-783-5000 • nmwa.org • $$ • Metro: Metro Center

■ NATIONAL POSTAL MUSEUM
Part of the Smithsonian Institution, the National Postal Museum is elegantly housed in the former Washington City Post Office, close by Union Station and designed by Graham and Burnham in 1914. The galleries, complete with interactive displays, explore topics such as the history of mail delivery, the passion of stamp collecting, the role of direct marketing, and the art of personal correspondence. A prop plane and a railway car are among the vintage modes of mail delivery on display in the 90-foot-high (27 m) atrium.

2 Massachusetts Ave., N.E. • tel 202-633-5555 • postalmuseum.si.edu • Metro: Union Station

■ CHARLES SUMNER SCHOOL
MUSEUM AND ARCHIVES
One of three historic public elementary schools for African-American children, and one of the District's few remaining

Classical and contemporary artists alike are represented in airy galleries within the National Museum of Women in the Arts.

landmarks devoted to early black history, the Charles Sumner School occupies a stately redbrick building erected in 1872. It's named for U.S. Senator Charles Sumner, a Massachusetts abolitionist who fervently fought for civil rights, including abolishing slavery in D.C. Slated for demolition in 1978, the building was saved by an organized community effort and today its museum and archives document the history of D.C.'s public schools.

1201 17th & M Sts., N.W. • tel 202-730-0478
• sumnermuseumdc.org • closed Sat.–Sun.
• Metro: Farragut North, Farragut West

■ HEURICH HOUSE MUSEUM
Washingtonians walk by this Romanesque Revival castle-like home never realizing they can view what's inside: the ornate abode of turn-of-the-20th-century German brewer Christian Heurich, one of the foremost brewers in local history. Heurich arrived in the United States a poor immigrant in 1866 and, having learned the brewing trade from his father, started a brewery. In time, Christian Heurich Brewing Company became Washington's second largest employer, after the federal government. When Heurich had this

house built (between 1892 and 1894), it was one of the city's first Gilded Age mansions. After his death, Heurich's descendants deeded the house to what became the Historical Society of Washington. A self-guided tour takes you through 11 rooms on three levels. Lavish decorations include a marble mosaic floor in the main hall, a Tiffany chandelier, and elaborately carved furniture in the dining room. Don't miss the beautiful Victorian garden.

1307 New Hampshire Ave., N.W.
• tel 202-429-1894 • heurichhouse.org
• closed Sun.–Wed.; call ahead for tour reservations • $ • Metro: Dupont Circle

■ KREEGER MUSEUM

Tucked away on 5.5 sculpture-dotted acres (2.2 ha) in the wooded Foxhall neighborhood of Northwest D.C., this private art museum showcases Impressionists and American artists from the 1850s to the 1970s, collected by insurance executive David Lloyd

DOWNTOWN

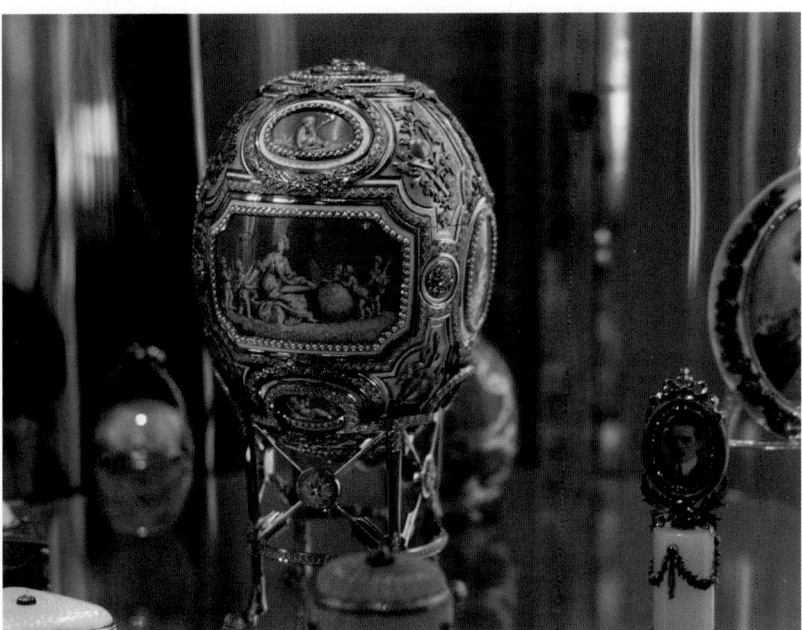

The Catherine the Great Easter Egg, crafted by Fabergé, at the Hillwood Museum

Kreeger and his wife, Carmen. Nine paintings by Claude Monet, a graceful Alexander Calder mobile hanging in the grand staircase, and a series of Picassos (the Kreegers' favorite artist) that trace his career are just a few of the highlights. The impressive collection also includes traditional art from Africa and Asia. The house alone is worth the visit—it's one of just a few examples in Washington, D.C., of work by postmodernist architect Philip Johnson. Classical and jazz concerts are sometimes offered after hours.

2401 Foxhall Road, N.W. • tel 202-337-3050 • kreegermuseum.org • Tues.–Thurs. by reservation only (tel 202-338-3552 or email visitorservices@kreegermuseum.org), Fri.–Sat. no reservation needed; closed Sun.–Mon. • $$ • Not Metro accessible

■ INTERNATIONAL SPY MUSEUM

Opened in May 2019 in a spacious new location, this fun, interactive museum sweeps you up into the shadowy world of espionage. Upon entering, you receive a cover identity and are tasked with maintaining your cover as you test your spy skills on an undercover mission. Find out as you learn about a spy's motives (politics, patriotism, money) and the skills, training, and expertise required for success. Real agents and spy catchers helped design the museum, with its thought-provoking exhibits on mass surveillance and interrogation, its underground spy tunnel from Berlin in the 1950s, plus exhibits ranging from a KGB "lipstick pistol" to James Bond's Aston Martin DB5 from *Goldfinger*. In fact, the sinister angular building, eerily lit by night, looks like a setting from a 007 movie.

700 L'Enfant Plaza • tel 202-393-7798 • spymuseum.org • $$$$$; reserve tickets in advance to avoid long lines • Metro: L'Enfant Plaza, Smithsonian

■ PRESIDENT LINCOLN'S COTTAGE

The 16th president spent summers during the Civil War at this 34-room Gothic Revival "cottage" about 3 miles (5 km) north of the White House's bustle, on the grounds of the Old Soldiers' Home. Here, surrounded by open green countryside, on one of the city's highest points, Lincoln could relax in the breeze—though it wasn't all fun and games. He orchestrated much of his Civil War business from here, including drafting the Emancipation Proclamation. Guided tours take you through the period-decorated rooms, telling tales of daily life.

140 Rock Creek Church Rd., N.W. • tel 202-829-0436 • lincolncottage.org • $$$ • Metro: Georgia Avenue–Petworth

White House
& Around

In 1791, architect and civil planner Pierre-Charles L'Enfant, under the direction of President George Washington, chose the site for the President's House— on a hill at one end of the city, about a mile from the future U.S. Capitol. Irish-born architect James Hoban drew the winning design, based on the Duke of Leicester's palace near Dublin. As the house was not ready for residents until 1800, John Adams was the first president to move in. The neighborhood grew in tandem, becoming a focus of political power and attracting such governmental edifices as the Eisenhower Executive Office Building and the Department of the Treasury, as well as the charming 18th-century town houses edging Lafayette Park. Today, intermingling with the official, are more approachable churches, luxury hotels, and art museums.

108 **Neighborhood Walk**

118 **In Depth:
White House**

122 **Distinctly D.C.:
Presidential
Washington**

124 **Best Of:
Secret Statues**

◀ **The aptly named
Red Room of the
White House, of late
used as a reception
room and to host small
dinner gatherings
with the president**

White House & Around

The People's House is the centerpiece of this stroll through Washington's historic heart.

⑤ National Geographic Society (see p. 112)
Exciting interactive exhibits delve into the successes of this foremost research and exploration institution. Backtrack down 17th St., N.W., cutting across Farragut Square to the corner of Pennsylvania Ave., N.W.

④ Decatur House (see pp. 111–112)
Learn about the life and times of the hero of the War of 1812, and those who came after him, in this beautifully curated historic house on Lafayette Square. Walk north on 17th St., N.W.

③ St. John's Episcopal Church (see pp. 111)
Find the pew reserved for presidents before crossing H St., N.W., and walking one block west.

⑥ Renwick Gallery (see pp. 112–113)
You'll be wowed by this Smithsonian museum's dedication to the future of art. Cross Pennsylvania Ave., N.W., and proceed south on 17th St., N.W., bearing right on New York Ave., N.W.

Map labels

2 Lafayette Square (see p. 110) Admire stately statues, relax on a shady bench, and get a different perspective on the White House from this lovely park. Then stroll to the square's north side.

Willard Inter-Continental — ⑩

14TH STREET

PENN. AVE. S.

PERSHING PARK

White House Visitor Center

Ellipse Visitor Pavillion

Sherman Statue

15TH ST.

PENN. AVE.

F ST.

MADISON PL. (no public access)

3 St. John's Episcopal Church

Hay-Adams Hotel — ④ Decatur House

② Lafayette Square

White House

① (closed to vehicles)

PRESIDENT'S PARK

Zero Milestone

The Ellipse ⑨

National Christmas Tree Site

Renwick Gallery — ⑥

Eisenhower Executive Office Building

STATE PL.

E STREET

17TH STREET

(no public access)

H STREET

17TH ST.

PENNSYLVANIA AVE.

G ST.

F ST.

NEW YORK AVE.

American National Red Cross

D STREET

E STREET

Octagon House ⑦

18TH ST.

C ST NW

Organization of American States ⑧ Art Museum of the Americas

1 White House (see pp. 118–121) Lucky you if you have tickets to visit the White House. If not, stop by the White House Visitor Center. Then head to Lafayette Square, just north of the White House across pedestrianized Pennsylvania Avenue.

0 100 meters
0 100 yards

7 Octagon House (see p. 114) This oddly shaped historic house has served more than once as the president's house. Proceed south on 18th St., N.W.

8 Art Museum of the Americas & Organization of American States (see pp. 114–115) Enjoy the small art gallery and relax in the secret indoor tropical garden—especially beloved in winter. Backtrack on 17th St., N.W., turning into the President's Park at State Pl., N.W.

9 The Ellipse (see p. 116–117) Stroll across this grassy expanse, site of the nation's Christmas tree, along with a fabulous view of the back of the White House. Continue across the Ellipse, making your way to 15th St., N.W., at Pennsylvania Ave., N.W.

10 Willard InterContinental (see p. 117) The legendary hotel is a great place to end your walk with a refreshing drink.

WHITE HOUSE & AROUND

WHITE HOUSE & AROUND   DISTANCE: 3.25 MILES (5.2 KM)   TIME: APPROX. 6 HOURS   METRO: FARRAGUT WEST, FARRAGUT NORTH, METRO CENTER

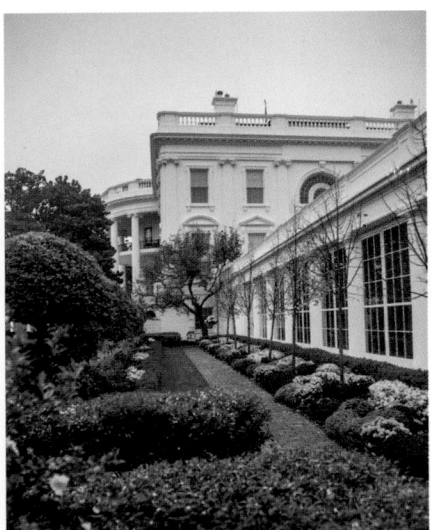

The Jacqueline Kennedy Garden flourishes outside the White House's east wing.

White House

1 See pp. 118–121.

White House: 1600 Pennsylvania Ave., N.W.; White House Visitor Center: 1450 Pennsylvania Ave., N.W. • tel 202-456-7041 • whitehouse.gov, nps.gov/whho • public tour requests must be submitted through your member of Congress three weeks to six months ahead of your visit • Metro: Federal Triangle, Metro Center, McPherson Square

Lafayette Square

2 This graceful, tree-shaded park facing the White House —with plenty of benches to rest your feet—has seen its share of demonstrations for or against something: nuclear disarmament, women's right to vote, or whatever is the political discord of the day. Part of the "President's Park" (though it lost the physical connection when Pennsylvania Avenue was cut through in 1804), the square centers on Clark Mills's **"Major Gen. Andrew Jackson"** on a rearing horse, the first cast-bronze equestrian statue made in the United States. On the park's four corners, statues of foreign-born Revolutionary War heroes include France's **"Marquis de Lafayette"** (southeast corner) and "**Comte de Rochambeau"** (southwest); Prussia's **"Baron Friedrich Wilhelm von Steuben"** (northwest); and Poland's **"Gen. Thaddeus Kosciuszko"** (northeast). Many of the fashionable 18th-century houses edging the square once housed Washington's elite; saved from the wrecking ball by a determined Jacqueline Kennedy, many today serve as White House offices.

North of the White House, H St. bet. 15th & 17th Sts., N.W. • tel 202-208-1631 • nps.gov/whho • Metro: McPherson Square, Farragut West

St. John's Episcopal Church

3 This little yellow stucco church across from the White House has hosted every president since James Madison for at least a bit of time—hence its nickname, Church of the Presidents. James Madison's wife, Dolley, was baptized and confirmed here, and Franklin Delano Roosevelt prayed here on both of his inauguration days. Designed by famed architect Benjamin Henry Latrobe (who helped design both the White House and Capitol), it opened its doors in 1816. Check out **Pew No. 54,** the President's Pew, reserved for the president should he or she decide to attend. Paul Revere's son Joseph cast the 1,000-pound (454 kg) bell in the steeple in 1822.

1525 H St., N.W. • tel 202-347-8766 • stjohns-dc.org • Metro: Farragut North, Farragut West, McPherson Square

GOOD **EATS**

■ **BREADLINE**
Yummy, healthy salads, soups, and sandwiches.
1751 Pennsylvania Ave., N.W., tel 202-822-8900, $

■ **FOUNDING FARMERS**
Eco-chic American cuisine using local ingredients.
1924 Pennsylvania Ave., N.W., tel 202-822-8783, $$–$$$

■ **TEAISM**
Asian-inspired light fare.
800 Connecticut Ave., N.W., tel 202-835-2233, $$–$$$

Decatur House

4 This historic home on Lafayette Square doubles as the David M. Rubenstein National Center for White House History, with enthralling stories about life in the early capital throughout a free guided tour. This three-story federal-style house was originally built for Commodore Stephen Decatur, Jr., naval hero of the War of 1812. Designed by famed architect Benjamin Henry Latrobe, it was completed in 1818—but Decatur barely had the chance to enjoy the place. He was killed in a duel with a fellow officer 14 months after moving in. His wife rented the house to the likes of Henry Clay and Martin Van Buren. Today visitors are taken across the elegant brick courtyard the parlor rooms and the ballroom, much of which emanate with the aura of a later owner, Mrs. Truxtun Beale, who presided over a salon for ambassadors and politicians. The tour ends in Washington's only extant slave quarters. If your schedule doesn't permit joining a tour, check the website for the interesting special exhibitions that take place in the parlor rooms. On Thursday evenings June through August, jazz musicians play under the stars in the beautiful courtyard; reserve tickets in advance.

Enter at 1610 H St., N.W. • tel 202-218-4300 • whitehousehistory.org • tours Mon., 11 a.m., 12:30 p.m., & 2 p.m.; check website for special exhibitions • Metro: Farragut North, Farragut West, McPherson Square

National Geographic Society

5 Established in 1888 to support the exploration of the world's farthest reaches, this revered institution has sponsored such big-name explorers as Jacques Cousteau, Jane Goodall, and Sylvia Earle. The main headquarters comprises the three buildings clustered here, home to the Society's flagship "yellow-bordered" magazine, as well as the National Geographic Channel, National Geographic Travel Books, National Geographic Expeditions, and Live! speaker series—and the list goes on. As you enter through the 17th Street entrance, look up to the ceiling between the elevators at the marvelous 3-D relief of the **Grand Canyon.** Then delve into the exhibits presented in the National Geographic Museum, with exhibits that include "National Geographic: Exploration Starts Here", regaling two centuries of exciting discoveries spanning nature, science, and adventure. There's always a free photography exhibit presented "beneath the stars" in the building across the courtyard (the stars represent how the night sky looked when the Society was founded in 1888). A lively lecture series, lunchtime films, and other events are available as well; check the website. If it's lunchtime, you can dine at the staff cafeteria, or grab a coffee or snack at the snack bar.

1145 17th St., N.W. • tel 202-857-7000 • nationalgeographic.com • $$$ • Metro: Farragut North, Farragut West

Renwick Gallery

6 The architecturally distinctive Renwick Gallery, dating from 1859, was the first public building in America designed specifically to showcase works of art to the public. Along these lines, the

Smithsonian American Art Museum used the building to display its contemporary craft program between 1972 and 2013. After an extensive two-year renovation a whole new chapter began when the museum reopened with a brand-new focus looking toward art in the 21st century and American genius. Mind-boggling exhibitions are the goal—the inaugural exhibit, for example, was called "Wonder" and focused on gallery-size installations including one room with walls full of intricate, spiraling, wallpaper-like designs—all made from dead bugs; green marbles flowing across a floor and up the walls to represent the Chesapeake; and the mold of a hemlock tree hollowed out and hand-carved to resemble the original tree. It's a magnificent look into the future of art.

1661 Pennsylvania Ave., N.W. • tel 202-633-7970 • renwick.americanart.si.edu • Metro: Farragut West, Farragut North

The Renwick Gallery hosts innovative American art such as Patrick Dougherty's "Shindig."

Octagon House

7 Standing bravely in the shadow of austere modern edifices, the Octagon House was built about the same time as the White House for a prominent Virginia planter, John Tayloe III, and his wife, Ann Ogle Tayloe. Designed by the first architect of the Capitol, Dr. William Thornton, and completed by 1801, it was the neighborhood's first private residence at a time when little else existed in the area. Its true claim to fame, however, is the role it served as the residence of James and Dolley Madison after the British burned the nearby President's House in 1814. Just a few months later, in February 1815, Madison signed the war-ending Treaty of Ghent in an upstairs parlor. Bought by the American Institute of Architects in 1902, it has been extensively renovated back to its Tayloe-era look. Take a self-guided tour through the sparsely decorated rooms—including the drawing room, dining room, upstairs parlors, Treaty Room/Study, and basement.

1799 New York Ave., N.W. • tel 202-626-7439 • architectsfoundation.org/preservation • open Thurs.–Sat. • Metro: Farragut West, Farragut North

Art Museum of the Americas & Organization of American States

8 The Organization of American States has two parts—an art museum, entered via 18th St., N.W., and the actual OAS building, entered around the block via 17th St., N.W. Begin with the small Art Museum of the Americas, showcasing rotating pieces from its permanent collection; traveling shows of Latin America and Caribbean art and photography take place as well. Don't miss the blue-tiled loggia, adorned in Aztec and Inca designs. Exiting, backtrack half a block to C St., N.W., turn right to 17th St., N.W., and right again, to the grandiose facade of the Organization of American States headquarters. The OAS is a regional alliance of 35 member countries from the Americas and the Caribbean promoting peace and economic cooperation among its members. Admire the building's striking mix of classical and Spanish Colonial architecture, proclaimed an architectural wonder when it

Organization of American States (OAS) building

opened in 1910 (architects Paul Cret and Albert Kelsey designed the building to represent the unity of the Americas by combining Spanish French, Portuguese, English, and indigenous influences). A statue of **"Queen Isabella the Catholic"** greets you in front, a reminder that Spain sponsored Christopher Columbus's travel that led to the European discovery of America. Guided tours are offered Monday to Friday by pre-arrangement. Right away you'll come to the lovely **tropical garden patio,** an oasis of rubber, fig, coffee, and banana plants centered on a pink marble fountain. President William Howard Taft planted the **Peace Tree,** a hybrid of fig and rubber, during the building's dedication ceremonies. Behind the garden, a hall hosts changing exhibits related to the Americas and the Caribbean. Climb the massive staircase to the second floor, where the **Hall of Flags and Heroes** greets you with flags of all OAS members, as well as busts of national heroes—including George Washington, Simón Bolívar, and José de San Martín. Finally, step into the adjacent, elegant **Hall of the Americas,** where the Panama Canal Treaties were signed in 1977.

Art Museum of the Americas: 201 18th St., N.W.; Organization of American States headquarters: 200 17th St., N.W.• tel 202-370-0735 • oas.org, museum .oas.org • $$$$$ • Metro: Farragut West

IN **THE KNOW**

The first Christmas tree gracing the Ellipse dates to 1923, when President Calvin Coolidge "pushed the button" to light a 48-foot (14.6 m) balsam fir from his home state of Vermont. Various trees were either lit elsewhere on the grounds or live ones were trucked in from other states until 1978, when a Colorado spruce from Pennsylvania was planted on the spot. (At the time of writing, the current tree is a Colorado spruce from Virginia.)

Every president continues the traditional rite of lighting the National Christmas Tree each year following a festive musical extravaganza. Smaller trees representing the fifty states, the District of Columbia, and U.S. territories, flank the bigger tree along the "Pathway of Peace," and model trains chug around in one of the city's most festive settings.
thenationaltree.org

Each year the large National Christmas Tree, ceremoniously lit by the president, is visited by some 400,000 people.

The Ellipse

9 On the White House's south side, the Ellipse is a 52-acre (21 ha) grassy area surrounded by an oval drive. Entering from 17th Street, N.W., at State Place, N.W., stroll up the walk to the iron fence guarding the South Lawn. From here, you get fabulous views of the back of the **White House.** The **Truman Balcony** was controversial when President Truman proposed it in 1947—the president arguing it was a needed solution to provide shade for the family, the purists stating such an atrocity would destroy the federal look of the exterior. Truman, of course, won, and today it's a lovely place for the first family to relax and entertain—and enjoy some of the house's best views out onto the Mall. The expanse of grass and garden flanking the White House, the **South Lawn** is where formal and informal ceremonies take place, including the Easter Egg Roll every spring. If you're lucky, you might spy a military helicopter—Marine One—buzzing overhead, bringing the president home. Tucked away among the foliage are a jogging track, a swimming pool, a basketball court, and a tennis court. If you turn around and face the other way, you'll see the **National Christmas Tree** that's decorated every holiday season, a tradition that began with

President Calvin Coolidge in 1923 (see sidebar opposite). Here, too, is the 4-foot-high (1.2 m) **Zero Milestone,** where all road distances in the United States were to originate. That never happened; instead, only roads in Washington, D.C., are measured from here. It's the best place to take a photo of the White House.

Just south of the White House • tel 202-208-1631 • nps.gov • Metro: Farragut West, Metro Center

Willard InterContinental

The story goes that the term "lobbyist" was first used at this grand, beaux arts–style hotel, when those seeking favors or inside information cornered presidents and politicians in the lobby. The truth is that the word was used long before, in reference to the House of Commons, but there's no doubt the Willard's importance as a meeting place invigorated the use of the term in the Capital City. Charles Dickens, Nathaniel Hawthorne, Harry Houdini, Mae West, and countless presidents, foreign dignitaries, literati, and glitterati have all been honored guests. During the Civil War, Julia Ward Howe wrote "The Battle Hymn of the Republic" in her room here; more than a hundred years later, Martin Luther King, Jr., added the finishing touches to his "I Have a Dream" speech while in the Willard's lobby. Established in the 1850s and rebuilt from the ground up in its current style in 1904, the hotel closed in mid-1968 after racial rioting following the assassination of Martin Luther King, Jr.; Congress saved it from demolition by designating it as a historic landmark. It reopened in all of its previous opulence in 1986. With three restaurants, the famed **Round Robin Bar** (likely the oldest operating bar in D.C.), and its proximity to the White House, the Willard has become a monument unto itself. At the very least, go in and admire its lavish lobby. Or step it up a notch and enjoy afternoon tea at **Peacock Alley** to the strains of harp music.

1401 Pennsylvania Ave., N.W. • tel 202-628-9100 • ihg.com • Metro: Metro Center

White House

See the official residence and workplace of the president of the United States, filled with treasures from presidents past and present.

Hannibal keeps watch over the White House Blue Room from a circa 1817 mantel clock.

Every U.S. president except George Washington has lived in this most famous of residences. The District of Columbia's oldest public building, its construction began in 1792 and was completed eight years later. In its 132 rooms, the president meets with national and foreign leaders, signs bills into law, hosts state dinners, briefs the press, all the while trying to lead a private family life. The only way for the general public to visit is by contacting your congressperson up to six months in advance to arrange a self-guided tour.

WHITE HOUSE & AROUND

You will be sent a timed ticket ahead of your visit (tours are Tue.-Sat.). Foreign visitors can request a tour through their embassy in Washington, D.C. Bring it at your appointed time to the south side of the East Executive Avenue entrance and go through a security check. Walk through the **East Colonnade,** adorned with historic photos of presidential life in the White House to the right; views onto the **South Lawn,** with the Washington Monument rising in the distance, are to the left. You then enter the ground floor of the White House.

■ LIBRARY

This pretty room was originally used as a laundry room, until President Theodore Roosevelt turned it into the servants' locker room in 1902. It became the official library in 1935, and ever since has held important tomes on American thought and tradition—2,700 to date. The room, tastefully decorated in late federal period style including furniture by New York cabinetmaker Duncan Phyfe, is often used for teas, press interviews, and small meetings.

■ EAST ROOM

Walk up the steps and enter the house's largest room, decorated in late 18th-century classical style. Here's where state dinners, receptions,

SAVVY **TRAVELER**

Even if you haven't been able to arrange a tour of the White House itself, the **White House Visitor Center** provides a fascinating introduction to life within the Executive Mansion. Interactive exhibits tell behind-the-scenes stories, including the usher's role, the evolution of the Oval Office, and surprising presidential menu requests (including Garfield's squirrel soup). Don't miss the video narrated by the president that adds personal notes of residents past and present of what it means to live in America's most famous residence.

dances, concerts, weddings, award presentations, press conferences, and bill-signing ceremonies take place. Union troops were quartered here during the Civil War, and this is where the bodies of Abraham Lincoln and John F. Kennedy were laid in state. First kids have taken a liking to its expanse as well—Tad Lincoln fashioned a sleigh out of a kitchen chair and two goats and took a ride across its Fontainebleau parquetry oak floor. Jimmy Carter's daughter, Amy, roller-skated here, leaving marks that weren't fixed for 30 years. And Abigail Adams hung her family's laundry in this unfinished room when she and John moved into the damp residence. Note the portrait of George Washington by

Gilbert Stuart—it's the same painting that Dolley Madison removed as the British descended to burn the White House in 1814, and thus it's the only piece in the White House that remains since its first occupancy in 1800.

■ GREEN ROOM

The first of three state parlors on the first floor, the Green Room has always been a popular place for small meetings and tea. Thomas Jefferson hosted dinners here, and here James Madison signed the nation's first declaration of war—the War of 1812. As part of her program to give the White House a more dignified, museum-like look, Jacqueline Kennedy selected its delicate green watered-silk fabric in 1962. Be sure to note the silver coffee urn, belonging to John and Abigail Adams; and the French candlesticks, owned by James and Dolley Madison.

■ BLUE ROOM

This elegant, elliptical-shaped room is the most formal of the parlor rooms, where the president officially receives kings and heads of state during receptions. James Monroe had the room decorated in the French Empire style in 1817—the seven gold chairs, the sofa, and the mantel clock date from that time. It was Martin Van Buren

who added the color blue, in 1837. Don't miss George P. A. Healy's 1859 portrait of John Tyler on the west wall, considered to be the finest in the series of presidential portraits. The principal White House Christmas tree sparkles in this room every year.

■ RED ROOM

The American Empire style popular in the early 1800s is striking in this opulently decorated room, though it's perhaps the vibrant red color—in the red twill satin fabric on the walls, as well as in the red-silk-and-gold-trimmed furniture—that hits you first. Theodore Roosevelt favored the Red Room as a smoking room, and today it continues to be used as an after-dinner parlor. The marble mantel has been in the White House since 1819.

■ STATE DINING ROOM

Designed in the style of neoclassical English houses of the late 18th century, the State Dining Room can host up to 140 guests at its mahogany dining table. When a state dinner is not in the works, the table is often adorned with James Madison's French Empire porcelain. George P. A. Healy's 1869 portrait of a contemplative Abraham Lincoln hanging over the fireplace was given to the White House by the family in 1939.

WHITE HOUSE & AROUND

The red carpet is ready to be rolled out for high occasions along the Cross Hall, connecting the State Dining Room with the East Room of the White House.

■ CROSS HALL & ENTRANCE FOYER

At the end of the tour, visitors are guided through the glistening marble floors and walls of the Cross Hall, which connects the State Dining Room with the East Room. A gallery of recent presidential portraits hangs from the walls, and the stunning cut-glass chandeliers were made in London about 1775. Join the line to take a selfie beneath the Presidential Seal, and then you are given the honor of leaving through the **Entrance Foyer** and out the official front door.

White House: 1600 Pennsylvania Ave., N.W.; White House Visitor Center: 1450 Pennsylvania Ave., N.W. • tel 202-456-7041 • whitehouse.gov, nps.gov/whho • public tour requests must be submitted through your member of Congress three weeks to six months ahead of your visit • Metro: Federal Triangle, Metro Center, McPherson Square

Presidential Washington

As you tour Washington, D.C., reminders are everywhere that you're on P.O.T.U.S.'s turf—the White House at 1600 Pennsylvania Avenue, N.W., of course, is the most obvious giveaway. But chances are, you'll also experience blocked streets, motorcades, and the excitement of the Marine One helicopter whirring overhead. Washington has been the president's town since the beginning—whether you like it or not.

Inauguration day brings out crowds of visitors to launch the new leader of the United States, from the solemn swearing-in on the steps of the Capitol (Barack Obama, 2013, above) to exuberant parades down Pennsylvania Avenue (Bill Clinton, 1993, opposite).

The President's House

The White House stands proudly behind iron gates, a draw for photo-snapping tourists from near and far. Through the years, the home and office of the president have become an enduring symbol of leadership and political freedom in America and around the world. The media's common attribution "according to the White House" shows how the physical house has become united with the ideals of the chief executive—and the nation that elected him or her—who resides within.

Inauguration Day

Every four years, Washington, D.C., decks itself out to welcome the new (or reelected) president, a tradition that began with George Washington in 1789, a week after he was inaugurated in New York City. The official swearing in takes place in front of the Capitol on the third Monday of January (a local holiday), with the entire Mall becoming packed with people who either watch with their naked eyes if they're close enough, or from the Jumbotrons positioned all along the Mall. Afterward, parties abound—there are several official inaugural balls, which you must *be* someone or *know* someone who's someone to get in. The president and first lady make a personal appearance at each one. But there are plenty of other parties for normal folk to attend too, sponsored by state societies, businesses, and private organizations.

Motorcades

The president always travels with his or her Secret Service motorcade—a long line of motorcycles, black SUVs, and police cars, all flashing lights and sirens for protection. Other dignitaries have motorcades too, of varying sizes; the car carrying a foreign dignitary will fly their national flag on the hood. You know it's the president's motorcade because an ambulance always trails behind . . . just in case.

THE PRESIDENTS' RACE **BASEBALL STYLE**

Should you attend a home game with the Washington Nationals baseball team, you'll witness the "Presidents' Race" in the middle of the fourth inning—pitting likenesses of up to six presidents (Washington, Jefferson, Lincoln, Theodore Roosevelt, Coolidge, and Taft), topped with giant caricature heads, against one another in a foot race around the outfield. There are no rules, and the winner is not necessarily predetermined. Pick your prez and cheer him on!

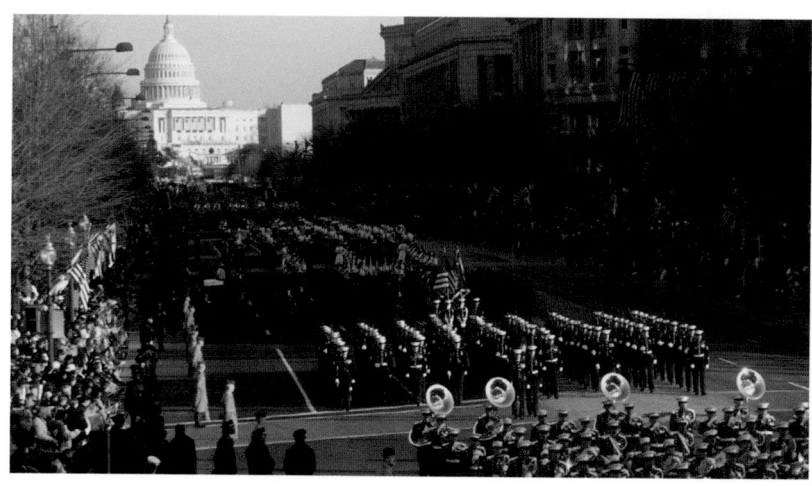

Secret Statues

Washington is filled with statues extolling noteworthy people and events throughout history. Here are some of the more intriguing, less obvious ones.

WHITE HOUSE & AROUND

■ EINSTEIN MEMORIAL
Looking like an overstuffed teddy bear, a rough-hewn, chunky, bronze sculpture of Albert Einstein by Robert Berks sits near the Mall on the grounds of the National Academy of Sciences, where the esteemed scientist became a member in 1942. The sculpture celebrates Einstein's three most important scientific contributions: the photoelectric effect, the theory of general relativity, and the equivalence of energy and matter. But perhaps the most endearing thing about this 12-foot (4 m) statue is that kids can climb up into his lap—an ingenious photo op!

National Academy of Sciences, 2101 Constitution Ave., N.W. • tel 202-334-2000 • Metro: Foggy Bottom–GWU

■ EMANCIPATION MEMORIAL
Dedicated on the 11th anniversary of Lincoln's assassination in 1876, the statue in Lincoln Park, on Capitol Hill, predates the more famous Lincoln statue on the National Mall. Here, a bronze President Lincoln stands proudly next to a kneeling, seemingly subservient former slave. Though heralded at the time of its creation, it has evolved into controversy; some feel the statue fails to show the role African Americans—including black Union soldiers—played in fighting for their own emancipation.

Lincoln Park, East Capitol St., S.E., bet. 11th & 13th Sts. • tel 202-690-5185 • Metro: Stadium–Armory

■ TITANIC MEMORIAL
This cinematic granite statue of an angelic man seemingly sailing through the air, head raised and arms extended, commemorates the men who gave their lives when the famous ship sank in 1912 so that the women and children could live. Gertrude Vanderbilt Whitney, American sculptor, art patron, and founder of New York's Whitney Museum of Art, designed the statue in 1931.

Washington Channel Park, near 4th & P Sts., S.W., along Southwest Waterfront • Metro: Waterfront

A suitably larger-than-life statue of T. R. Roosevelt hails visitors to Roosevelt Island.

■ THEODORE ROOSEVELT ISLAND NATIONAL MEMORIAL

It will take a little doing to find the only statue in the nation's capital dedicated to the 26th president of the United States—but it's worth it. Head to Theodore Roosevelt Island in the Potomac River across from Georgetown. Surrounded by woods, the Great Conservationist no doubt would have loved his position here.

Northern tip of Theodore Roosevelt Island, accessible via the pedestrian footbridge just north of Roosevelt Bridge or via a walkway south of Key Bridge, both on the Virginia side of the Potomac River • tel 703-289-2500 • nps.gov/this • Metro: Rosslyn

■ ADAMS MEMORIAL

Sculptured by the renowned artist Augustus Saint-Gaudens, this haunting statue honors Clover Adams, wife of Henry Adams, who committed suicide in 1885. Adams commissioned the sculptor to create a memorial that would capture the Buddhist notion of Nirvana. It can be tough to find; look on a hillside in the cemetery's eastern end. Another option is to see a reproduction in the Smithsonian American Art Museum (see pp. 96–98).

Rock Creek Cemetery, St. Paul's Episcopal Church, 201 Allison St., N.W. • tel 202-726-2080 • rockcreekparish.org • Metrobus: 60, H8

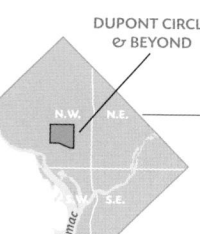

Dupont Circle & Beyond

Taking in an enticing mix of neighborhoods, this walk begins at Dupont Circle, centered around a lovely marble fountain. Back in the 1870s, the surrounding neighborhood, called Pacific Circle, drew society's crème de la crème—mining, steel, and shipping tycoons who held elaborate receptions and musicals in their beaux arts mansions. Today, simply strolling the streets and admiring these homes is a delight. You'll also find cafés, galleries, and small museums, notably the nationally acclaimed Phillips Collection. Nearby 14th Street is a hotbed of hip restaurants, bars, and boutiques. Just north, U Street takes on a more bohemian attitude, sprinkled with African-American landmarks. And north from here, Adams Morgan is a colorful Latino realm with more small shops, restaurants, and bars— with Ethiopian influences mingled in as well.

128 **Neighborhood Walk**

136 **In Depth:
The Phillips Collection**

138 **Distinctly D.C.:
Multicultural
Washington**

140 **Best Of:
World of Festivals**

◀ **Rear Admiral Samuel
Francis Dupont
Memorial Fountain**

Dupont Circle & Beyond

Start this walk through some of D.C.'s diverse Northwest neighborhoods a little later in the day, so you can take full advantage of the evening offerings.

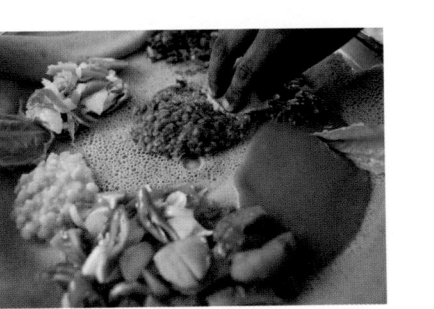

6 U Street, N.W. (see pp. 133–134) **Bohemia meets ethnic diversity meets Harlem Renaissance on this eclectic street alive with restaurants, clubs, and shops, plus some important African-American landmarks. Stay on U St., N.W., following it west to 18th St., N.W.**

7 Adams Morgan (see pp. 134–135) Explore bookshops, global cuisine, and coffee shops by day, hopping bars and salsa-imbued lounges by night in this favorite multicultural neighborhood.

① Dupont Circle
(see pp. 130–131)
A gracious fountain-centered circle in the heart of a residential neighborhood serves as a meeting place for all walks of life. Go up Connecticut Ave., N.W., to Q St., N.W., and turn left, to 21st St., N.W.

② The Phillips Collection
(see pp. 136–137) A small house museum with big-bang exhibits, both permanent and temporary. Backtrack down 21st St., N.W., to Massachusetts Ave., N.W., and turn right.

③ Anderson House (see pp. 131–132) Learn about the Society of the Cincinnati, the secretive patriotic organization whose first president general was none other than George Washington, in this unassuming mansion. Continue up Massachusetts Ave., N.W., and turn right on S St., N.W.

④ President Woodrow Wilson House (see p. 132) See inside one of the neighborhood's poshest homes, and learn about the 28th president at the same time. Continue east on S St., N.W., to 14th St., N.W., and turn left (though there are interesting things to see to the right as well).

⑤ 14th Street, N.W.
(see pp. 132–133) Shop, eat, and drink your way through this booming area between Rhode Island Ave. and U St., N.W., then amble north to U St., N.W.

DUPONT CIRCLE & BEYOND   DISTANCE: 2.5 MILES (4 KM)
TIME: APPROX. 5 HOURS   METRO: DUPONT CIRCLE

Map labels: President Woodrow Wilson House ④ · African American Civil War Memorial and Museum · 14th Street N.W. ⑤ · The Phillips Collection ② · Cosmos Club · Anderson House ③ · Dupont Circle ① · SHERIDAN CIRCLE · Rock Creek · 14TH ST · 15TH ST · 16TH ST · 17TH ST · 18TH STREET · 19TH STREET · 21ST ST, N.W · 23RD ST · NEW HAMPSHIRE · CONN. AVE · FLORIDA AVE · MASS. AVE · LEROY PL · BANCROFT PLACE · DECATUR PLACE · S ST · R STREET · Q ST · P ST · T STREET · SWANN · RIGGS PLACE

Dupont Circle

1 Standing in the midst of tree-shaded Dupont Circle, a pocket-size green haven surrounded by the whiz of traffic, you get a glimpse of L'Enfant's vision of public space—a gift to the citizens of a fledgling democratic nation. Indeed, Dupont Circle is a magnificent meeting space for an egalitarian cross section of suits, uniforms, jeans, and cutoffs. In the middle rises the majestic marble fountain sculpted in 1921 by Daniel Chester French (also known for the giant statue of Lincoln in his memorial on the National Mall). A central column supporting the upper basin is surrounded by three allegorical figures representing the sea, wind, and stars. Honoring Civil War naval hero Samuel Francis du Pont, the fountain replaced a statue of du Pont that originally stood there. Grab a cup to go from a nearby coffee emporium and enjoy some of the city's finest people-watching, or take advantage of the built-in

Intricately woven tapestries line an upstairs hallway of the sumptuous Anderson House, longtime home to the Society of the Cincinnati.

chessboard tables and grassy plots under trees, an open invitation for lounging. Nearby, **Kramerbooks & Afterwords Café** *(1517 Connecticut Ave., N.W., tel 202-387-3825)* is a favorite local bookstore worth some good browsing time.

Intersection of Massachusetts Ave., N.W., Connecticut Ave., N.W., New Hampshire Ave., N.W., P St., N.W., & 19th St., N.W. • Metro: Dupont Circle

The Phillips Collection

2 See pp. 136–137.

1600 21st St., N.W. • tel 202-387-2151 • phillipscollection.org • closed Mon. • $$$ • Metro: Dupont Circle

IN **THE KNOW**

Washington's art scene has been stealthily gaining strength, with galleries flourishing all over town. Get to know Dupont Circle's ring of galleries the first Friday of every month when their doors open to all, live music and wine included. Start and end at the **IA&A at Hillyer** *(9 Hillyer Ct., N.W.)*.

Anderson House

3 Enter this enormous 1905, 50-room mansion—once called a "Florentine villa in the midst of American independence"—and you enter another world. It was once the winter residence of diplomat Larz Anderson III; his heiress wife, Isabel Weld Perkins, gave the mansion to the Society of the Cincinnati, of which he was a member, upon his death in 1937. It now serves as the society's headquarters and museum. Strolling through the richly decorated rooms, showcasing a mix of artifacts related to the society and the Andersons' outstanding fine and decorative arts collection, you learn the story of this fraternal patriotic organization, dating from 1783. Today's 3,500 members descend from officers in the Continental Army or Navy—indeed, the first president general was George Washington himself.

On the **first floor** you'll find walnut choir stalls dating from 16th-century Italy as well as a two-story-high ballroom with red Verona marble columns. Off the ballroom, a sun-drenched winter salon opens onto a walled garden. On the **second floor** Flemish tapestries in both the luxuriant French drawing room and the formal dining room are among the many treasures adorning the walls.

President Woodrow Wilson standing on the porch of his home, 1922

Historians note: The 40,000-title research library focuses on the art of 18th-century warfare.

2118 Massachusetts Ave., N.W. • tel 202-785-2040 • societyofthecincinnati.org • closed Mon. • Metro: Dupont Circle

President Woodrow Wilson House

④ Get a peek inside another neighborhood home at this lovely Georgian Revival mansion, where the 28th president lived for the three years before his death in 1924. His widow, Edith Bolling Galt Wilson, lived here until her death in 1961, then bequeathing the house—along with much of its furnishings, portraits, books, and artifacts related to the Wilson Administration—to the National Trust for Historic Preservation. Today it appears much as it did when the Wilsons resided here, complete with Woodrow's walking sticks and Edith's gowns in their closets. The artillery shell on his bedroom mantel is said to be the first fired by American forces in World War I.

2340 S St., N.W. • tel 202-387-4062 • woodrowwilsonhouse.org • closed Mon. year-round & Tues.–Thurs. in winter; by guided tour only, on the hour • $$ • Metro: Dupont Circle

14th Street, N.W.

⑤ The best part about 14th Street is checking out the latest and greatest along the corridor of bars, restaurants, boutiques, antique shops, and theaters between Rhode Island Avenue and U Street on this, one of D.C.'s most happening streets. National names in fashion, cuisine, and theater are also drawn here. Just wander, poke your head into doorways, and see what you come across. Shopping is

DUPONT CIRCLE & BEYOND

fun and funky at **Salt & Sundry** (*605 14th St., N.W., tel 202-621-6647*), full of bath and kitchen goodies. **Current Boutique** (*1809 14th St., N.W., tel 202-588-7311*) offers forward-trending female fashion from designers around the world. And **Miss Pixie's** (*1626 14th St., N.W., tel 202-232-8171*) has bookshelves plus silver and textiles and other treasures bought directly at auction.

For eats, the Gulf-style **Pearl Dive Oyster Palace** (*1612 14th St., N.W., tel 202-319-1612*) gives you oysters any way imaginable; the Black Salts are grown specially in Virginia for chef Jeff Black. **B Too** (*1324 14th St., N.W., tel 202-627-2800*) is a hopping contemporary Belgian restaurant that goes above and beyond the standard endive salad and waffles. The ever popular **Le Diplomate** (*1601 14th St., N.W., tel 202-332-3333*), a quintessential Parisian-style bistro slash café, is chef Stephen Starr's entrée to 14th Street, with great people-watching on the patio. And then there's aviation-themed **Café Saint-Ex** (*1847 14th St., N.W., tel 202-265-7839*), one of the neighborhood's longest standing ventures (founded in 2003). Named for Antoine de Saint-Exupéry, an avid pilot and author of *Le Petit Prince*, the down-to-earth eatery is French in look, but with a decidedly eclectic Americana menu.

14th St., N.W., bet. Rhode Island Ave. & U St. • Metro: U Street–African-American Civil War Memorial–Cardozo

U Street, N.W.

6 Another hopping street scene, U Street is experiencing phoenix-like growth in an area that deteriorated after the 1968 riots following Martin Luther King's assassination. Before then, in the late 19th and early 20th centuries, this was a prestigious address, home to the city's leading black intellectuals and professionals. People donned their finest attire to frequent the restaurants, movie theaters, pool halls, and dance halls of

GOOD **EATS**

See also individual entries.

■ **HANK'S OYSTER BAR**
A longtime neighborhood favorite, with an ever changing oyster menu. **1624 Q St., N.W., tel 202-462-4265, $$–$$$**

■ **LAURIOL PLAZA**
Popular, three-level Tex-Mex restaurant, with Latin American and Spanish added to the mix. **1835 18th St., N.W., tel 202-387-0035, $$**

■ **TABARD INN RESTAURANT**
New American cuisine in an old town house. **1739 N St., N.W., tel 202-931-5137, $$$**

Black Broadway and be entertained by such local stars as Edward Kennedy "Duke" Ellington and Pearl Bailey. Pay homage to these sights, clustered in and around the junction of 14th Street and U Street, N.W., and enjoy some of the offbeat shops along the way. **Cultural Tourism DC** *(1211 U St., N.W., tel 202-355-4280, culturaltourismdc.org)* offers guided heritage walking tours of the neighborhood; stop by their office next to Ben's Chili Bowl.

Other neighborhood highlights include the **African American Civil War Memorial and Museum** *(Memorial: U St. & Vermont Ave., N.W.; Museum: 1925 Vermont Ave., N.W., tel 202-667-2667, afroamcivilwar.org, museum closed Mon.)*, dedicated to the African-American troops who fought in the Union Army; exhibits at the museum include photos, newspaper articles, and reproductions of period clothing, uniforms, and weaponry. Big-name gigs have returned to the beautifully restored **Lincoln Theatre** *(1215 U St., N.W., tel 202-888-0050, thelincolndc.com)*, dating from 1935. And don't forget to stop by **Ben's Chili Bowl** *(1213 U St., N.W., tel 202-667-0909, benschilibowl.com)* next door for a late-night cup of famous chili. This spicy dog and chili joint—seemingly the only place that has stayed the same through the neighborhood's radical changes—has been a frequent stop since 1958 for those in the know, including such celebrities as Duke Ellington, Bono, and President Barack Obama.

U St., N.W., bet. 9th & 18th Sts. • Metro: Shaw–Howard U, U Street–African-American Civil War Memorial–Cardozo

Adams Morgan

7 This down-to-earth, energetic neighborhood centering on the junction of Columbia Road with 18th Street, N.W., unveils a culturally diverse mélange of noteworthy offerings: from Ethiopian restaurants to salsa bars to global boutiques. Long a Latino enclave and a popular late-night drinking venue among young Washingtonians, the neighborhood has been reinventing itself into a more chichi, craft-cocktail type of destination. That said, enough of the multicultural character still remains. Grab a cup of coffee at a European-style café, peruse one of the many art galleries and small shops, and take your pick of places to dine on international cuisine. If you're lucky to be here during the Adams Morgan Day Festival on the second Sunday of September (see p. 140), you'll get an insider's look at what it's all about. Favorite hangouts for locals and visitors alike include **Perry's** *(1811 Columbia Rd., N.W., tel 202-234-6218, perrysam.com)*, a Japanese restaurant with coveted rooftop bar and popular Sunday drag-queen brunch; **Songbyrd** *(2477 18th St., N.W., tel 202-450-2917, songbyrddc.com)*, purveyors of vinyl music; and **District of Columbia Arts Center** *(2438 18th St., N.W., tel 202-462-7833, dcartscenter.org, closed Mon.–Tues.)*, an art gallery for up-and-coming artists that also hosts a theater. If you're still hungry, **Mintwood Place** *(1813 Columbia Rd., N.W., tel 202-234-6732, mintwoodplace.com)* is a foodie destination, with **Julia's Empanadas** *(2452 18th St., N.W., tel 202-328-6232, julias empanadas.com)* being a walk-in favorite.

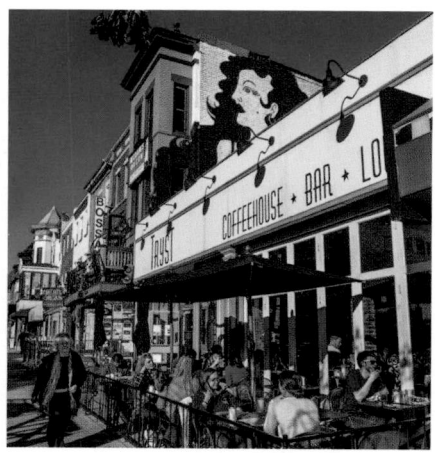

A lively food scene flavors Adams Morgan.

And if you come here for the nightlife, be sure to check out **Jack Rose Dining Saloon** *(2007 18th St., N.W., tel 202-588-7388, jackrose diningsaloon.com)*, a high-end bar noted for its whiskeys; the unforgettably named **Madam's Organ** *(2461 18th St., N.W., tel 202-667-5370, madamsorgan.com)*, a lively blues bar and soul food restaurant; and **Habana Village** *(1834 Columbia Rd., N.W., tel 202-462-6310, habana village.com)*, with salsa lessons offered most days for a modest fee.

Intersection of Columbia Rd. & 18th St., N.W. • Metro: Woodley Park–Zoo–Adams Morgan

The Phillips Collection

World-class masterpieces in a welcoming space await art lovers at America's first museum of modern art.

The Phillips's oak-paneled Music Room has hosted Sunday afternoon concerts since 1941.

This delightful small museum, which art patron Duncan Phillips established in 1921 based on his personal collection, reigns as the nation's first modern art museum. Intimate rooms occupying Phillips's 1897 Georgian Revival brownstone and a contemporary addition showcase works by Cézanne, van Gogh, Picasso, Gauguin, Klee, and others—with the most celebrated piece being Renoir's dazzling "Luncheon of the Boating Party." But Phillips collected lesser known artists as well—you'll discover them interspersed throughout.

■ Special Exhibits

The Phillips curates blockbuster temporary exhibitions. Start your visit on the third floor with the latest show.

■ Renoir's Masterpiece

A small set of stairs leads to the room holding Pierre-Auguste Renoir's famous "Luncheon of the Boating Party," an explosion of light and color. Phillips fell in love with the painting—and paid $125,000 in 1923, at a time when seven-room homes in Georgetown sold for $6,500.

■ Laib's Wax Room

Nearby, a single bulb hangs in a small gold-hued room covered with fragrant beeswax, the creation of conceptual artist Wolfgang Laib.

■ A Room Full of Rothko

The Rothko Room was designed to the precise aesthetic specifications of both the abstract expressionist Rothko and Phillips—a rare collaboration between artist and patron. Four large paintings featuring Rothko's signature rectangles of color hang here, enveloping viewers in a saturation of hues.

SAVVY **TRAVELER**

As you stroll through the museum, keep in mind you won't necessarily find installations based on geography or chronology. Instead, the museum has fun with how it hangs the works—centering on unique themes such as windows or similar still lives by different artists.

■ Lawrence's "Migration Series"

The Phillips owns the odd-numbered paintings of Jacob Lawrence's "Migration Series," which depict the migration of African Americans from the rural South to the urban North during and after World War I. The paintings are moved around the museum, so keep an eye out for them.

■ Music Room

A perennial favorite, this oak paneled room with its decorative ceiling and carved mantelpiece has hosted Sunday afternoon concerts since 1941 (*Oct.– May; seating first-come, first-served*).

■ A Bit of Fresh Air

Before leaving, take a rest on the benches of the outdoor courtyard as you ponder the open-air sculptures.

DUPONT CIRCLE & BEYOND

1600 21st St., N.W. • tel 202-387-2151 • phillipscollection.org • closed Mon., Sunday p.m. concerts Oct.–May • $$$ • Metro: Dupont Circle

Multicultural Washington

You could say Washington was created by a French man. Indeed, Pierre-Charles L'Enfant is responsible for the noble, tree-shaded, Euro-style urban design that graces the nation's capital—roundabouts, broad boulevards, lots of fountains and statues, stone buildings, and a grand parklike mall included. Since those early days, Washington has welcomed people from around the world—foreign delegations, of course, but also others in search of a better way of life, bringing with them their cultures, cuisines, and traditions.

Drumming at Meridian Park (above) and international restaurants (opposite) are but two of the hundreds of ways that Washington's ethnic diversity is celebrated and shared with residents and visitors alike.

In the Beginning

L'Enfant aside, Washington was not so ethnically diverse in the beginning. Indeed, in 1900, only 7 percent of the population was foreign-born, compared to New York's 37 percent, Boston's 35 percent, and Philadelphia's 23 percent. Today, about 1 in 7 Washingtonians are foreign-born.

Abroad at Home

Throughout the Washington area, you'll find neighborhoods where various ethnic groups have settled, establishing shops, restaurants, and businesses to support their communities, celebrating traditions and annual festivals—and offering a way for everyone to experience the world at home.

Chinatown is one of the oldest neighborhoods, established in the 1930s. Restaurants and shops cluster in the hopping Penn Quarter neighborhood, where a colorful Friendship Arch spans over H Street and the Chinese New Year parade unfurls.

The years following the Vietnam War saw an influx in Vietnamese. The Eden Center strip mall in the D.C. suburb of Falls Church, Virginia, offers 100-plus Vietnamese bakeries, restaurants, groceries, and shops. An annual Tet Festival attracts thousands with food, fireworks, live entertainment, and lion dances.

Washington boasts what is believed to be the world's second largest Ethiopian population, after Addis Ababa; many Ethiopians sought asylum in the United States as a result of Ethiopia's civil war in the 1990s. Little Ethiopia is found along U Street between 13th and 9th Streets, N.W. Among Latinos, you'll find every Central and South American country represented throughout the Washington region, with El Salvadoreans claiming the highest representation. Adams Morgan is historically the heart of the Latino community, where you'll still find *pupuserias* and salsa clubs. And the list goes on and on.

INTERNATIONAL RESTAURANTS

Here are some of D.C.'s best ethnic restaurants.

Las Canteras (Peruvian) 2307 18th St., N.W., tel 202-265-1780

Bombay Club (Indian) 815 Connecticut Ave., N.W., tel 202-659-3727

Brasserie Beck (Belgian) 1101 K St., N.W., tel 202-408-1717

Dukem Ethiopian Restaurant, 1114–1118 U St., N.W., tel 202-667-8735

Lebanese Taverna 2641 Connecticut Ave., N.W., tel 202-265-8681

Mandu (Korean) 453 K St., N.W., tel 202-289-6899

Mari Vanna (Russian) 1141 Connecticut Ave., N.W., tel 202-783-7777

DUPONT CIRCLE & BEYOND

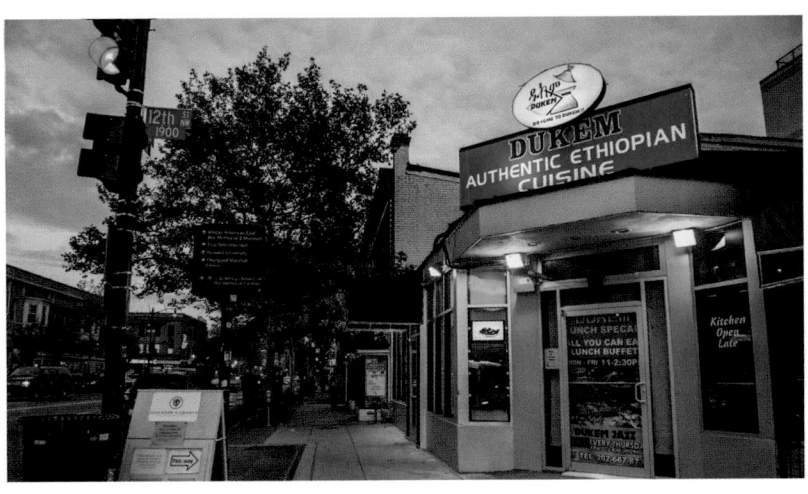

World of Festivals

Experience Washington's tapestry of different cultures, celebrated throughout the year with extravagant music, parades, dance, and—always—lots of good food.

■ ADAMS MORGAN DAY

Since 1978, on the second Sunday of September, the streets of the traditionally Latino Adams Morgan are blocked off for the eclectic neighborhood festival, complete with live music, international food, and an **International Dance Plaza** featuring all kinds of dance performances, including Bolivian and Mexican folk—and the chance to learn some basic moves yourself.

18th St., N.W., bet. Florida Ave. & Columbia Rd. • admoday.com • second Sun. in Sept.

■ DRAGON BOAT FESTIVAL

Vibrantly colored dragon boats race on the Potomac River in an ancient Chinese tradition that also includes cultural exhibits, food, and music. The two-day festivities kick off with the **Eye-dotting Ceremony** to awaken the sleeping dragon boats. For the best vantages, head to the Washington Harbour and Georgetown Riverfront Park.

Thompson Boat Ctr., 2900 Virginia Ave., N.W. • tel 202-333-9543 • dragonboatdc.com • May

■ FIESTA DC

This annual extravaganza of Latino heritage has become so big that it's been moved downtown from the Columbia Heights neighborhood. The highlight is the **Parade of Nations,** featuring more than 30 folkloric groups from Spain, Latin America, and Mexico sashaying down Constitution Avenue. Other **Festival Latino** events include a children's festival, science fair, and plenty of international cuisine.

Parade of Nations: Constitution Ave., N.W., bet. 7th & 14th Sts.; Festival Latino: Pennsylvania Ave., N.W., between 9th & 14th Sts. • tel 202-290-2335 • fiestadc.org • Sept.

■ ST. PATRICK'S DAY PARADE

Bagpipers—plus 100 marching bands, military units, dance schools, floats, and more—march down Constitution Avenue in this enormous annual tradition going on for more than 45 years. Grandstand tickets are available for a price.

Constitution Ave., N.W., bet. 7th & 17th Sts. • tel 202-670-0317 • dcstpatsparade.com • Sun. near St. Patrick's Day

Honduran dancers during the Parade of Nations, Fiesta DC

■ NATIONAL CHERRY BLOSSOM FESTIVAL

A four-week celebration with the famous blooms as its centerpiece. See pp. 64–65 for more information.

Tidal Basin & surrounds • tel 877-442-5666 • nationalcherryblossomfestival.org

■ SMITHSONIAN FOLKLIFE FESTIVAL

The Smithsonian's Center for Folklife and Cultural Heritage spotlights several different cultures from around the world in this massive, dynamic festival on the National Mall. Hundreds of artisans, chefs, musicians, and storytellers entertain thousands with demonstrations, talks, and concerts, with overall themes and countries highlighted each year. Try to arrive early to avoid the crowds; it's always hot—drink plenty of water.

National Mall • tel 202-633-6440 • festival.si.edu • weekends nearest Fourth of July

■ SCOTTISH CHRISTMAS WALK WEEKEND

Hundreds of Scottish clansmen with tartans and bagpipes parade through Old Town Alexandria in this annual December event. Other activities include a historic homes tour, a Celtic party, and Christmas marketplace.

King St., Old Town Alexandria • tel 703-549-0111 • campagnacenter.org • first Sat. in Dec.

Georgetown

Centering on Gothic-spired Georgetown University, Washington's superchic neighborhood mixes posh shopping and energetic nightlife with quiet streets lined by refined federal and Victorian architecture. It began as a tobacco inspection shipment port on the highest navigable point along the Potomac River. The colony of Maryland established a town here in the 1750s, naming it for George II. Georgetown became a thriving trade center, with stately merchant houses spangling the hill, and artisans' shops and warehouses along the riverside. Georgetown's blacksmiths, cabinet-makers, carpenters, and other artisans supported the fledgling Federal City with materials to build the White House and other federal buildings in the late 1700s. The city of Washington annexed Georgetown in 1871. Among the busy shops and restaurants you'll find such historic landmarks as the C & O Canal and Old Stone House, along with genteel manses and lovingly maintained gardens that provide a glimpse into yesteryear, Tudor Place, and Dumbarton House among them.

144 **Neighborhood Walk**

152 **In Depth:
     Dumbarton Oaks**

154 **Distinctly D.C.:
     Spies Among Us**

156 **Best Of: Gardens**

◐ The Chesapeake and Ohio (C & O) Canal stretches some 184.5 miles (297 km) from Cumberland, Maryland, to Washington, D.C., passing through Georgetown. Its scenic towpath is much enjoyed by locals.

Georgetown

Brick row houses along tree-shaded streets, pocket gardens, and award-winning eateries are just a few of the charms of this historic neighborhood.

7 Tudor Place Historic House & Garden (see p. 149) Six generations of the same family lived here. Continue up 31st St., N.W., turn left on R St., N.W., and right on 32nd St., N.W.

8 Dumbarton Oaks (see pp. 152–153) This historic house has a hidden gem of a museum, plus formal gardens designed by landscape architect Beatrix Farrand. Backtrack on R St., N.W.

6 Cox's Row & Around (see p. 149) Admire more stately federal homes on a picturesque cobbled street. Continue on N St., N.W., to 31st St., N.W., and turn left to Q St., N.W.

5 Georgetown University (see p. 148) Stroll the grounds of America's first Catholic university, dating from 1789. Exiting campus, turn right on 37th and left on N St., N.W., to 34th St., N.W.

4 Prospect Street, N.W. (see pp. 147–148) Gaze at gorgeous historic homes. Turn right at 37th St., N.W., to O St., N.W., and the entrance to Georgetown University.

**GEORGETOWN   DISTANCE: 3.3 MILES (5.3 KM)
TIME: APPROX. 6 HOURS   METRO: FOGGY BOTTOM–GWU**

Dumbarton Oaks

8

MONTROSE PARK

Oak Hill Chapel & Cemetery

9

Rock Creek

R ST.

9 Oak Hill Chapel & Cemetery (see p. 150) The final resting place of some of Washington's most famous movers and shakers. Continue on R St., wrapping around to 28th St., N.W., then turning left on Q St., N.W.

32ND ST.

31ST ST.

Tudor Place Historic House & Garden

7

Q ST.

WISCONSIN

P ST.

O ST.

N ST.

30TH ST.

29TH ST.

28TH ST.

10 Dumbarton House (see pp. 150–151) A fascinating glimpse into Georgetown's early history through the eyes of one family. Attend an evening concert or other special event in the historic house.

Dumbarton House

10

Q ST.

1 Old Stone House (see p. 146) Visit Washington's oldest house, then head down Thomas Jefferson St., N.W., to the canal, and turn left.

St. John's Church

AVENUE

Martin's Tavern

GEORGETOWN

PROSPECT STREET

Old Stone House

1

STREET

M. STREET

The Shops at Georgetown Park

Blues Alley

Chesapeake & Ohio Canal

GRACE ST.

SOUTH ST.

WISCONSIN AVE.

31ST ST.

CECIL PL.

T. JEFFERSON ST.

Georgetown Visitor Center for C & O Canal

CHESAPEAKE & OHIO CANAL NATIONAL HISTORICAL PARK

2

WHITEHURST FWY. (elevated)

29

Potomac

GEORGETOWN WATERFRONT PARK

Washington Harbour

3

Rock Creek

30TH ST.

Thompson Boat Center

2 Chesapeake & Ohio Canal National Historical Park (see p. 146) After stopping by the Georgetown Visitor Center, head west along this 184.5-mile (297 km) historic towpath. In summer you can take a mule-drawn barge ride. Stroll to 31st St., N.W., and turn left to Washington Harbour.

3 Washington Harbour (see p. 147) Bustling restaurants and bars with a riverside view—this is the perfect place for lunch. Walk north along Georgetown Waterfront Park to 34th St, N.W., up the steps, over the canal, then up through Francis Scott Key Park. Crossing M St., N.W., go left to 35th St., N.W., and walk up the steep hill.

0   200 meters
0   200 yards

Old Stone House

1 Washington's oldest house (dating from 1766), the Old Stone House has through the years served as a house painter's shop, clockmaker's shop, antiques store, and the offices of a used-car dealership. The legend that George Washington slept here—though since disproved—helped keep it from demolition. The federal government bought the house in 1953 to preserve its history, and today it provides a glimpse into ordinary Georgetown life before the founding of the Capital City. Poke your head inside to see the kitchen, parlor, and bedrooms furnished as in the late 18th century. Out back, a colonial revival garden contains roses, perennials, and bulbs.

3051 M St., N.W. • tel 202-895-6070 • nps.gov/olst • Metro: Foggy Bottom—GWU

Chesapeake & Ohio Canal National Historical Park

2 George Washington dreamed of a canal that would connect the Atlantic coast with the Ohio River and he was the first president of the Patowmack Company, organized in 1785. Bankrupt, the Patowmack was succeeded in 1828 by the C & O, which built a canal as far as Cumberland, Maryland, and used it to transport grains, tobacco, whiskey, furs, and timber until railroads drove it out of business in the early 20th century. Thanks in large part to the conservationist clout of Supreme Court Justice William O. Douglas, the canal was saved from death by highway in the 1950s. Today it's a beautiful national historical park, a long, skinny recreation area that gets wilder the farther northwest you go—you can hike, bike, or walk the entire 184.5 miles (297 km) to Cumberland, though a short wander will also give you a nice respite. Stop at the **Visitor Center** in Georgetown for a free walking tour of the neighborhood or an hour-long ride in a reproduction of a **canal boat** from the 1800s—pulled by live mules!—that combines a pleasant excursion with a narrative on the canal's history and construction.

Visitor center: 1057 Thomas Jefferson St., N.W. • tel 202-653-5190 • nps.gov/choh • canal rides: seasonal; visitor center: closed winter • canal ride: $ • Metro: Foggy Bottom—GWU

Enjoying a meal at Washington Harbour, where Georgetown meets the Potomac River

Washington Harbour

3 In warm weather, this wide promenade hugging the Potomac River's northern shore becomes a prime Georgetown hot spot. Stop for lunch or a drink in an open-air restaurant (Sequoia is one of the more popular, with a tree-shaded terrace); or relax on a bench to enjoy close-up views of the river as well as leafy Roosevelt Island (dead ahead) and the sleek Kennedy Center (to the left). Just north along the Potomac, **Georgetown Waterfront Park** offers a beautiful riverside stroll toward the Key Bridge's graceful arches.

3050 K St., N.W. • tel 202-295-5007 • thewashingtonharbour.com • Metro: Foggy Bottom–GWU

Prospect Street, N.W.

4 This lovely, tree-shaded street boasts some of Georgetown's oldest and most fashionable houses, dating back to a time when wealthy shipowners, merchants, and land speculators built mansions above the three-masted-schooner-filled harbor. At the corner of 34th

GEORGETOWN

IN **THE KNOW**

Georgetown's chic row houses have long been coveted by the rich and famous. Jacqueline and John F. Kennedy are perhaps the most celebrated residents—JFK had seven Georgetown addresses until moving into 3307 N St., N.W., with Jackie; from here they went on to the White House. Elizabeth Taylor, as wife of Senator John Warner, lived at 3240 S St., N.W. Julia Child resided on Olive Street, N.W. There are plenty of high-level officials living on these leafy streets today; their addresses are unpublished, but the Secret Service agents standing guard are a dead giveaway.

and Prospect, No. 3400 identifies the federal-style **Halcyon House** (1787) built by Benjamin Stoddert, a Revolutionary War hero and the first secretary of the Navy. It served as a center of the young capital's social life—Dolley Madison danced here at the wedding of Stoddert's daughter. Today it serves as a creative space for 21st-century problem solvers. A few houses away stands **Worthington House** (No. 3425), built in 1798 by prominent landholder John Thomson Mason; the 24-paned windows lining both main floors cost a mint at the time. Just past 35th Street, at No. 3508, **Prospect House** (1788–1793) is a late Georgian beauty built by a Revolutionary War officer and outspoken advocate of freedom of the press.

Prospect St., N.W., bet. 34th & 35th Sts. • All private • Metro: Foggy Bottom–GWU

Georgetown University

5 When Georgetown opened in 1789, it was the United States' first Catholic university. The Gothic-spired university is best known for its schools of law, medicine, and foreign service (and its basketball team). Through the main gate you'll see **Healy Hall,** the historic flagship building named after Father Patrick Healy, an African-American priest and president of Georgetown in the 1870s. Note the hands on the clock tower, the object of many student pranks over time. Every five or six years (or whenever they can pull off the stunt), students steal these hands and mail them to the Vatican; the Vatican simply stamps "return to sender" and the package is returned to the university. Filled with students, the 104-acre (42 ha) campus is a pleasant place for a stroll; permanent maps sprinkled about the grounds help guide the way.

3700 O St., N.W. • tel 202-687-0100 • georgetown.edu • Metro: Foggy Bottom–GWU

Cox's Row & Around

6 Col. John Cox, the future mayor of Georgetown, built this grouping of stately federal-style brick town houses *(3327 to 3339 N St., N.W.)* around 1818. Cox entertained the Marquis de Lafayette at **No. 3337** during his U.S. visit in 1824. John F. and Jackie Kennedy lived at **No. 3307** between 1957 and 1961, before moving into the White House.

3300 block of N St., N.W. • Metro: Foggy Bottom–GWU

The pleasing facades of Cox's Row are little changed since their construction in the 19th century.

GEORGETOWN

Tudor Place
Historic House & Garden

7 Six generations of the Peter family—relatives of George Washington and Robert E. Lee—resided in this grand neoclassical mansion, which looks as if the family is still living here. Indeed, all of the furniture, porcelain, and decorative objects are original, reflecting the family's 178-year continuity between 1805 and 1983. Personal belongings include 253 pieces from Mount Vernon (look for the chairs from George's war headquarters and Martha's tea table), an etching of the Marquis de Lafayette that he himself presented when he was entertained here, and Francis Scott Key's desk. One-hour tours by experienced guides provide fascinating details about the Peter family, as well an overview of the architect—William Thornton, first architect of the U.S. Capitol, who incorporated a rare, full "temple" into the two-story stuccoed main building. Be sure to leave time to visit the gardens (see p. 156), which are among Georgetown's loveliest.

1644 31st St., N.W. • tel 202-965-0400 • tudorplace.org • by guided tour only, on the hour; closed Mon. & Jan. • $$ • Metro: Foggy Bottom–GWU

Dumbarton Oaks

8 See pp. 152–153.

Museum: 1703 32nd St., N.W.; Gardens entrance: R St. at 31st St., N.W. • tel 202-339-6401 • doaks.org • Museum: closed a.m. & Mon.; Gardens: closed Nov.–mid-March & a.m. • Gardens: $$ • Metro: Foggy Bottom–GWU, Dupont Circle

Oak Hill Chapel & Cemetery

9 One of the prettiest cemeteries anywhere, on a hillside overlooking Rock Creek Park, Oak Hill is the final resting place for some of Washington's greatest notables, including former Secretary of State Dean Acheson as well as Phillip and Katharine Graham (former publishers of the *Washington Post*). There are doctors, lawyers, politicians, and generals galore, as well as a Confederate spy or two. Founded in 1849 by philanthropist and art collector William Wilson Corcoran (who's also buried here), its iron entrance gates and English Gothic Revival chapel were designed by James Renwick, architect of the Smithsonian Castle. Buy a map at the gatehouse.

3001 R St., N.W. • tel 202-337-2835 • oakhillcemeterydc.org • Metro: Foggy Bottom–GWU, Dupont Circle

GOOD **EATS**

■ **1789 RESTAURANT**
Fine dining in a federal period town house. **1226 36th St., N.W., tel 202-965-1789, $$$$$**

■ **BOOEYMONGER**
Creative sandwiches are the hallmark of this local chain. **3256 Prospect St., N.W., tel 202-333-4810, $**

■ **MARTIN'S TAVERN**
The oldest family-run restaurant in Washington, D.C., since 1933. **1264 Wisconsin Ave., N.W., tel 202-333-7237, $$–$$$**

Dumbarton House

10 A meticulously and lovingly restored tribute to early Georgetown, this federal-style house-museum (built in 1800) tells the story of the 1804–1813 time period through the eyes of a local family. Joseph Nourse, who worked as the Register of the Treasury in the new federal government, moved here from Philadelphia with his wife when Georgetown had just been incorporated into the District of Columbia. Treasures abound throughout the mansion, but perhaps what is most amazing is the thoroughness of the restoration—the historic accuracy of the carpeting,

GEORGETOWN

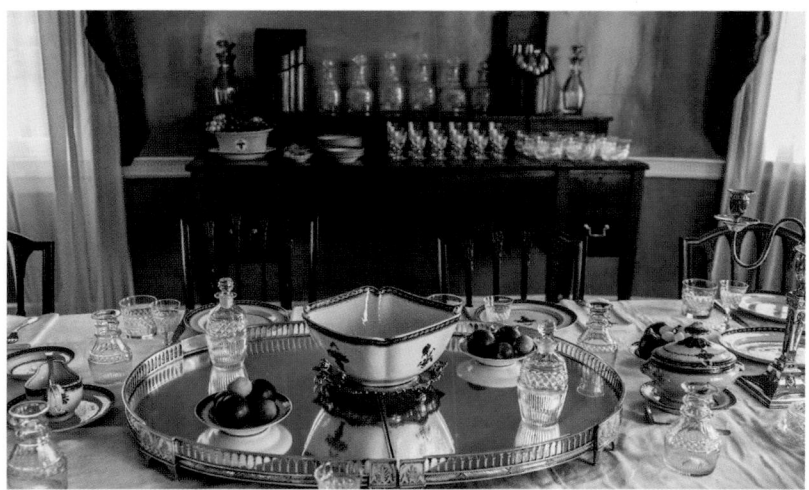

Dumbarton House's Chinese export blue-and-white porcelain dinner service dates from 1790.

the window dressings, the wallpaper, all reproduced based on original research, matching styles, colors, and methods of the day (and yes, early Americans did love their colors so bright!).

Keep an eye out for several outstanding artifacts, including Charles Willson Peale's painting "The Benjamin Stoddert Children" (1789) in the breakfast room, its background depicting early Georgetown; the porcelain dinner service that once belonged to Martha Washington's granddaughter in the dining room; and the rare schoolgirl needlework in the parlor. The second floor contains four galleries, one exploring the story of the National Society of the Colonial Dames of America, which curates the house and is headquartered here. Both self-guided and guided tours are offered; if you have time, a guided tour is highly recommended. After, take the self-guiding brochure for a peek at the small formal courtyard and garden. Special evening concerts happen on occasion; check the website for details.

2715 Q St., N.W. • tel 202-337-2288 • dumbartonhouse.org • by guided (Sat. & Sun.) & self-guided (Feb.-Dec.) tour; closed Mon. • $ • Metro: Dupont Circle

Dumbarton Oaks

*Discover the treasures beyond the famous gardens
at this exquisite Georgetown gem.*

Ornate baroque lines grace the pebble garden at Dumbarton Oaks, one of many lovely
botanical displays created by master landscape architect Beatrix Farrand.

Many Washingtonians know—rightly so—about the luxuriant gardens at

Dumbarton Oaks, designed by celebrated landscape architect Beatrix Farrand.

But few take the time to step inside the lavish, federal-style home, where

you'll find one of the world's most important small museums of Byzantine

and pre-Columbian art. Collected by Mildred and Robert Woods Bliss, this

impressive display is now curated by Harvard University. Here, too, the 1944

conference was held to charter the United Nations. The museum is free;

you'll have to buy a ticket to visit the gardens.

■ Byzantine Collection
Begin at the **Byzantine Courtyard Gallery** and the adjacent **Byzantine Gallery,** with artifacts spanning the 4th to the 15th centuries. The Blisses were especially captivated by the intricate detail work and fine craftsmanship of small objets d'art, which you'll find reflected in the gold, silver, and bronze vessels used for the celebration of the Eucharist, late Roman and Byzantine jewelry, coins, cloisonné enamels, and illuminated manuscripts. The neighboring **Textile Room** has rotating exhibits.

■ House Collection
The stately **Music Room,** designed in 1928 by the architectural firm of McKim, Mead & White and displaying a gorgeously painted wood-beamed ceiling, showcases the so-called House Collection. Exquisite tapestries and paintings hang on the walls—including El Greco's **"Visitation"** from the early 17th century. The 1926 **Steinway concert grand piano** is signed by Ignacy Paderewski. An exhibit gives a quick history on the Dumbarton Oaks Conference, which took place in this room.

SAVVY **TRAVELER**

Dumbarton Oaks is a self-guided visit, but a variety of different tours are available for those wanting to dive deeper. Some of the offerings include a **special exhibition tour**, a **historic rooms tour** (including the hall, Founders' Room, Study, and Oval Room), an **architecture tour**, and an **introductory garden tour.** Check *doaks.org* for more details.

■ Pre-Columbian Collection
A glass-and-travertine wing, inspired by Islamic architecture and designed by Philip Johnson, features circular galleries of glistening display cases arranged by region. These hold treasures from Latin America's ancient cultures, such as sparkling gold pectorals, ceremonial jewelry, and stone carvings of Aztec deities and animals.

■ The Gardens
Begin in the orangerie, where an entwining ficus plant from the 1860s festoons the walls and ceiling. Then wander through the gardens—a sweet-smelling realm of brick paths, boxwoods, perennial borders, iron gates, and balconies.

GEORGETOWN

Museum: 1703 32nd St., N.W.; Gardens entrance: R St. at 31st St., N.W. • tel 202-339-6401 • doaks.org • Museum: closed a.m. & Mon.; Gardens: closed Nov.–mid-March & a.m. • Gardens: $$ • Metro: Foggy Bottom–GWU, Dupont Circle

Spies Among Us

Intrigue. Mystery. Romance. Spies have captured the imagination of moviegoers and television-watchers for decades. But in Washington—home of the CIA, the FBI, and the Pentagon—such cinematic fare is real, with city streets very possibly alive with secret agents seeking or supplying classified information. Indeed, Washington boasts more spies than any other city in the world. You never know who you can trust!

GEORGETOWN

When Soviet KGB colonel Vitaly Yurchenko (above) returned to the Soviet Union in 1985 after defecting to the United States, many wondered if he was a KGB plant all along. His story, and many others, is told at the International Spy Museum (opposite).

Civil War Espionage

Spying caught on in Washington during the Civil War, when amateur agents on both sides of the Mason–Dixon line scoured the Capital City for war-related information. The city's most romantic spy may have been intelligent, beautiful, and duplicitous Rose O'Neal Greenhow (1815–1864), who frequented Washington's loftiest social circles. At one dinner party, after learning the Federals were planning to move into Virginia, she quickly passed a coded message to Confederate Gen. Pierre G. T. Beauregard inside a woman's hair bun, enabling him to reposition some of his troops—and, ultimately, to win the First Battle of Bull Run.

Cold War Spies & Beyond

Soviet KGB colonel Vitaly Yurchenko made world headlines when he strolled into the U.S. Embassy in Rome in August 1985 and stated he wished to defect. But Yurchenko was not a happy decamper, kept under close watch and relegated to a prisonlike existence. In November Yurchenko slipped his CIA handler and grabbed a cab to the Soviet Embassy. Four days later he was on a plane back to the Soviet Union. Then came Aldrich Ames, who in 1994 was accused of exposing U.S. intelligence assets inside the former Soviet Union. The info swap occurred at the now-defunct Chadwicks, at 3205 K Street in Georgetown; Ames chalkmarked a blue mailbox on R Street at 37th Street as a dead-drop signal. For his tip-offs, Ames received more than $2.7 million from the Soviets—and from the Americans, a life-long prison sentence.

Today spying is largely about tracking terrorist activities—the U.S. keeping tabs on Iran, North Korea, China, and the Islamic State. All of which no doubt are returning the favor.

HOW TO SEE— AND BE—**A SPY**

Rosanna Minchew, a retired CIA intelligence operative, leads espionage-themed walking tours of Georgetown *(airbnb.com/experiences/ 1122478)*, focusing on tales of intrigue throughout the Capital City. To try your own hand at intelligence activities, check out Operation Spy at the International Spy Museum (see p. 105).

GEORGETOWN

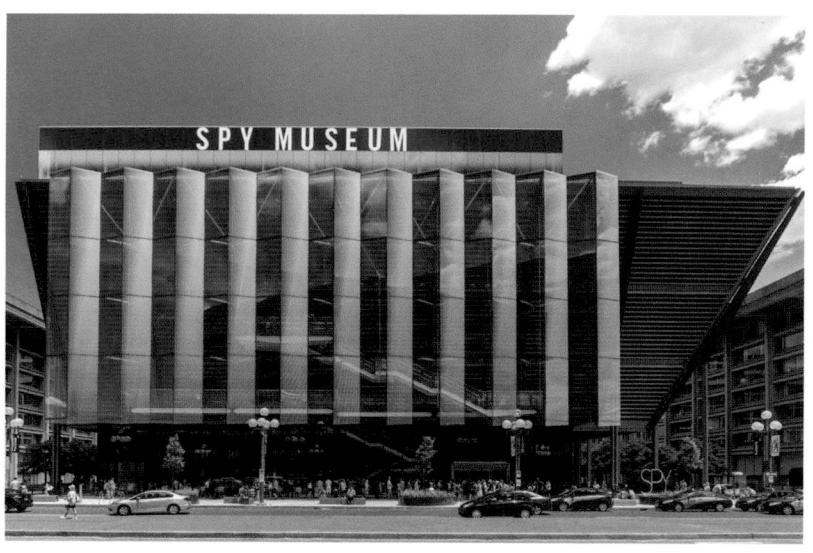

Gardens

Since Washington's earliest days, gardens have always had an important place in homes and public spaces alike—for practical purposes, but for beauty, too. Here are just a few of the beautiful spaces found throughout the city.

In springtime, keep an eye out for garden tours—including at the White House!

GEORGETOWN

■ TUDOR PLACE HISTORIC HOUSE & GARDEN

Tudor Place's quiet acres in the heart of Georgetown represent one of the nation's last intact urban estates from the federal period. Explore the sweeping **South Lawn** framed by 200-year-old trees, a **Box Knot Garden** featuring a "flower knot" pattern of English boxwoods and pathways, and the natural woodland settings. A garden map is available.

1644 31st St., N.W. • tel 202-965-0400 • tudorplace.org • closed Mon. & Jan. • $ • Metro: Foggy Bottom–GWU

■ U.S. BOTANIC GARDEN

Inside the iron-and-glass greenhouse on the Capitol grounds, more than 4,000 seasonal, tropical, and subtropical plants flourish—ranging from pineapple-scented sage to a plant that smells like rotting corpses. Established in 1820 and run by Congress, the garden's role through the ages has been to accumulate plants from military and exploring missions, foreign governments, states, and government agencies. Be sure to climb the stairs to the overhanging walkway in the large tropical atrium, filled with orchids and other epiphytes.

100 Maryland Ave., S.W. • tel 202-225-8333 • usbg.gov • Metro: Federal Center SW

■ FLORAL LIBRARY

On a site close to the famed cherry blossoms, some 10,000 tulip bulbs are planted by hand, later exploding in a vibrancy of springtime color. They are flown in every year from Holland to represent nearly 100 different varieties, explaining why this is called the Tulip Library as well. The rest of the year, annuals provide a sweet break from urban bustle. Established in 1969, the library was part of Lady Bird Johnson's effort to beautify the Capital City.

Just off Tidal Basin, east of Katz Bridge & south of Independence Ave., S.W. • nps.gov/nama • Metro: Smithsonian

The Rosary Portico frames the peaceful formal gardens of the Franciscan Monastery.

■ FRANCISCAN MONASTERY

One of Washington's best-kept secrets, tucked away on the grounds of a neo-Byzantine church, this oasis of peace in Northeast's Brookland neighborhood features lovingly executed reproductions of Holy Land shrines—the Grotto of Gethsemane, Chapel of the Ascension, the Tomb of Mary, plus the Lourdes grotto—all amid a parklike garden. Here, too, cloisters enclose a formal rose garden with benches thoughtfully placed for quiet contemplation. Check the website for a blooming calendar and to schedule tours of the monastery.

1400 Quincy St., N.E. • tel 202- 526-6800
• myfranciscan.org • Metro: Brookland–CUA

■ RIVER FARM

Overlooking the Potomac River south of Old Town Alexandria, en route to Mount Vernon, River Farm's landscaped grounds cover property that once belonged to George Washington. Among its meticulously maintained gardens are a small grove of Franklin trees (extinct in the wild), an orchard of pear, apple, and plum trees, and an azalea garden with hundreds of different kinds of azalea species. This beautiful setting is the headquarters of the American Horticultural Society.

7931 E. Boulevard Dr., Alexandria
• tel 703-768-5700 • ahsgardening.org
• open Mon.–Fri. April–Sept., plus Sat. a.m. Oct.–March • Not Metro accessible

Old Town Alexandria

Long before any notion of Washington, D.C., existed, Alexandria, Virginia, was a thriving colonial hotbed, known intimately by such patriots as Paul Revere, Thomas Jefferson, and, of course, nearby Mount Vernon resident George Washington. They worshipped at Christ Church, dined (and imbibed) at Gadsby's Tavern, and some even plotted wartime activity at the Carlyle House. Today, this quiet little realm of brick town houses, cobbled streets, and historic sites, located along the Potomac about 10 miles (16 km) downstream of Washington, is a delightfully strollable destination, easily reachable from D.C. by the Metro's blue line. Here, too, you'll find some of the region's most lauded bars, restaurants, cafés, art galleries, and boutiques—and a buzzing nightlife, especially in summer.

160 Neighborhood Walk

170 In Depth:
Christ Church

172 Distinctly D.C.:
Colonial Alexandria

174 Best Of:
Living History

◑ The former torpedo factory along Alexandria's waterfront is now a thriving arts center where more than 165 artists create, exhibit, and sell their work.

Old Town Alexandria

Older than Washington, charming Old Town Alexandria offers a step back into colonial days.

OLD TOWN ALEXANDRIA

❾ Torpedo Factory Art Center (see p. 169) Visit local potters, painters, and weavers as they purvey their arts and crafts in this former World War II torpedo factory. Then relax with some entertainment on the dock behind, overlooking the Potomac.

George Washington Masonic National Memorial ❻

❼ Lyceum, Alexandria's History Museum (see pp. 167–168) Get a primer on Alexandria's history, from Native American settlements to the present day. Backtrack to King St., turn right, then right on S. Fairfax St.

❽ Stabler-Leadbeater Apothecary Museum (see pp. 168–169) George Washington himself would recognize this pharmacy dating from colonial days. Continue down King St. to the Potomac River.

OLD TOWN ALEXANDRIA DISTANCE: 3.45 MILES (5.5 KM)
TIME: 8 HOURS METRO: KING ST.–OLD TOWN

1 Alexandria Visitor Center at Ramsay House (see p. 162) Enjoy breakfast at one of King Street's many cafés then begin your walk at this reconstruction of the 1724 home of town founder William Ramsay, now serving as the city's visitor information center. Go north on N. Fairfax St.

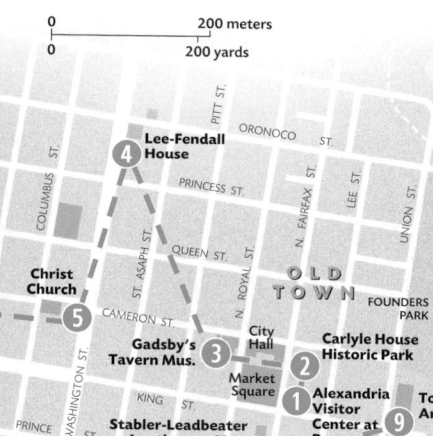

2 Carlyle House Historic Park (see pp. 162–163) Learn about one of Alexandria's earliest families at this colonial-era house, where British generals also plotted their strategy for the French and Indian War. At Cameron St., turn left and walk one block.

3 Gadsby's Tavern Museum (see pp. 163–164) Visit this historic tavern, then dine at the restaurant as the colonists did. Go north on N. Royal St., then left at Oronoco St.

4 Lee-Fendall House (see p. 165) Tours provide insight into the Lee family dynasty. Turn left on N. Washington St.

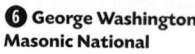

Map labels:
- 0 / 200 meters
- 0 / 200 yards
- PITT ST.
- ORONOCO ST.
- Lee-Fendall House (4)
- PRINCESS ST.
- COLUMBUS ST.
- ST. ASAPH ST.
- N. FAIRFAX ST.
- LEE ST.
- UNION ST.
- QUEEN ST.
- N. ROYAL ST.
- OLD TOWN
- Christ Church (5)
- CAMERON ST.
- FOUNDERS PARK
- N. WASHINGTON ST.
- City Hall
- Carlyle House Historic Park (2)
- Gadsby's Tavern Mus. (3)
- Market Square
- KING ST.
- Alexandria Visitor Center at Ramsay House (1)
- Torpedo Factory Art Center (9)
- Stabler-Leadbeater Apothecary Mus.
- PRINCE ST.
- WATERFRONT PARK
- Potomac
- PRINCE ST.
- Captain's Row
- (7)
- (8)
- Lyceum, Alexandria's History Museum
- S. FAIRFAX ST.

6 George Washington Masonic National Memorial (see pp. 166–167) Admire the view from the top of this majestic temple at the head of King St., where a small museum sheds light on the Masons. Then go back down King St. to N. Washington St. and turn right.

5 Christ Church (see pp. 170–171) Washington, Jefferson, and other patriots worshipped at this Anglican church. Go ahead and sit in Washington's pew, then exit onto N. Washington St., turn right, then right on King St. Walk the 1.3 miles (2 km) or take a cab to the temple.

Alexandria Visitor Center at Ramsay House

1 After enjoying breakfast at one of King Street's many cafés, stop by the city's visitor center for maps and some brochures to help plan your visit. While you're at it, take a good look at the architectural details of this meticulous reconstruction of the circa 1724 home of Scottish merchant and town founder William Ramsay. Be sure to check out special events on offer, including ghost tours and candlelit tours. The "Key to the City" pass available here offers a discount on various museum entry fees.

221 King St., Alexandria • tel 703-838-5005 • visitalexandriava.com
• Metro: King St.–Old Town

Carlyle House Historic Park

2 Scottish merchant John Carlyle completed this stone manse in the Georgian style in 1753, when Alexandria consisted mostly of small dwellings and warehouses. Soon, the French and Indian War pitted the British against the French and Indians, and Gen. Edward Braddock requisitioned the house for strategic planning with five colonial governors—he went on to be killed in battle in Pennsylvania. Today, guided tours begin every half-hour with an introduction providing historical context into the life and times of the Carlyle family. You will be greeted by your tour guide in the central passage (the best place in the house to catch a cool breeze in summer) and travel back in time to the 18th century. The first floor offers the main bedchamber, which has three original pieces of furniture, including a majestic four-poster bed and a lovely 1750 chest. Nearby is Carlyle's study, where he ran his mercantile business and which served as a private family space as well. You'll be taken through the parlor and formal dining room before heading up the main staircase to the second floor. Life in early America unveils itself with such details as the spinet harpsichord, similar to one played by Carlyle's daughter (who took lessons at Mount Vernon); fancy dinner place settings; and the popular green wallpaper so à la mode in the day (you'll find it at Mount Vernon and Dumbarton

Shops and restaurants vie for attention on Alexandria's King Street.

House as well). Exhibits on the second floor convey the life and times of various eras in Carlyle House's history, such as during the Civil War, when it was subsumed into a Union hospital known as Mansion House Hospital. Don't miss artifacts on display belonging to the real-life characters who inspired the public television series "Mercy Street," which delves into the everyday lives of Alexandrians during the Civil War.

121 N. Fairfax St., Alexandria • tel 703-549-2997 • nvrpa.org • $ • by guided tour only; closed Mon. • Metro: King St.–Old Town

Gadsby's Tavern Museum

3 Step into this beautifully preserved colonial-era public house and you might very well expect to find Thomas Jefferson, John Adams, James Madison, or any number of other early patriots imbibing as they discuss the social, political, and economic issues of the

OLD TOWN ALEXANDRIA

IN **THE KNOW**

As you walk from Gadsby's Tavern to the Lee-Fendall House, keep an eye out for the **"Spite House"** at 523 Queen St. The skinniest house in America, it measures just 7 feet (2 m) wide! John Hollensbury built it in 1830 to keep loiterers out of his adjacent alley.

day. It's known that George Washington would stop here between trips to and from his home at Mount Vernon. Consisting of a 1785 tavern and a 1792 hotel, Gadsby's has been faithfully restored as a museum and operating restaurant. The 30-minute tour takes you to the taproom, dining room, ballroom, assembly room, and third-floor communal bedchambers. As you admire the beautifully reproduced woodwork in the ballroom, remember that George Washington was honored here at the annual Birthnight Ball in 1798 and 1799; that Thomas Jefferson celebrated his inaugural banquet here in 1801; and that the Marquis de Lafayette was welcomed here on his American visit in 1824, at what was heralded as "one of the most brilliant of banquets." A visit to the period **Gadsby's Tavern Restaurant** (*138 N. Royal St., tel 703-548-1288, gadsbystavernrestaurant.com*) may bring peanut soup, Gentleman's Pye (lamb and beef in a red-wine stew topped with whipped potatoes and pastry crust), what's called George Washington's favorite (grilled breast of duck with scalloped potatoes and corn pudding), and other colonial-era specialties. Outside, peer into the subterranean ice well, built to assure a regular supply of ice—and year-round ice cream with flavors including vanilla, oyster, and parmesan; the dark paving stones on the corner of Royal and Cameron Streets mark the well's perimeter. En route to your next stop, take a glance at the frame house standing a block west at **508 Cameron Street.** George Washington built a town house on this very spot, including a stable and other necessary buildings, where he often stayed when visiting town prior to the Revolutionary War. While that house has been demolished, the current dwelling was built based on a contemporary drawing, and some believe that Washington's kitchen was incorporated into the nearby house at 506 Cameron, dating from 1817.

134 N. Royal St., Alexandria • tel 703-746-4242 • gadsbystavern.org
• $$ • museum by guided tour only; closed Mon.–Tues. Nov.–March
• Metro: King St.–Old Town

Lee-Fendall House

4 Lawyer Philip Fendall, cousin of Gen. "Light Horse Harry" Lee and husband of a distant aunt of Robert E. Lee, built this wood-frame house in 1785—the first of 37 Lees to reside here over the next 118 years. George Washington, one of Fendall's closest friends, dined here at least seven times. It's believed that Light Horse Harry Lee, who spent a great deal of time with the Fendalls, wrote his moving eulogy to George Washington here, penning the famous words describing the great man: "first in war, first in peace, and first in the hearts of his countrymen." Confederate general Robert E. Lee grew up across the street and no doubt stopped by to visit his cousins here as well.

Robert E. Lee, legendary general of the Confederate Army

The only way to see inside the house today is by guided tour, offered at the top of the hour; it takes you through the various rooms, furnished in the Victorian style of the 1850s through 1870s and showcasing family portraits, letters, and books. Keep an eye out for period pieces by local manufacturers. The fiery United Mine Workers leader John L. Lewis was the final resident of the home, between 1937 and 1969, and an interesting exhibit in one of the rooms honors him.

Even if you don't have time for a tour, you are free to relax—and even eat your picnic lunch—in the award-winning garden, with its towering magnolia and chestnut trees. From here you can also see how the house's vernacular "telescopic" architectural style works—the building is actually composed of several sections, each piece progressively smaller than the last; the Gothic Revival and Italianate flourishes were added later.

614 Oronoco St., Alexandria • tel 703-548-1789 • leefendallhouse.org • by guided tour only; closed Mon.–Tues. • $ • Metro: King St.–Old Town

Christe Church

5 See pp. 170–171.

118 N. Washington St., Alexandria • tel 703-549-1450
• historicchristchurch.org • Metro: King St.–Old Town

George Washington Masonic National Memorial

6 Rising 333 feet (101 m) on the hill at the head of King Street, the Masonic Temple, as it's called locally, is dedicated to George Washington, first president of the United States and the first of 14 U.S. presidents to be Masons. The Freemasons—a secretive fraternal organization that began in the 16th or 17th century within Scotland's stonemason guilds—built the ten-story shrine in the 1920s. They fashioned it after the Alexandria Lighthouse in Egypt to symbolize Washington's role as the guiding light of the American Republic, as well as to spread the "light and knowledge of Freemasonry to the world." Fans of the film *National Treasure* especially will appreciate the eclectic collection of artifacts found within. The one-hour tour lingers a bit on Masonic history, but it is worthwhile for the good collection of Washington memorabilia, including his family Bible, leather field trunk, and Clock of Death (the pocket watch stopped by Washington's physician at the moment of his death). The tools the doctor used to bleed Washington to death are also on display. The **Knights Templar Chapel** on the eighth floor is designed in medieval French Gothic style, with four beautiful stained-glass windows and an exquisite hand-crafted copy of the **Ark of the Covenant** inside a fake treasure room. From the open-air **observation deck** on the top of the tower (reached by elevator—which ascends at a 7-degree angle), all of Alexandria and beyond sprawls before your eyes. Be sure to take a look at the Masonic square-and-compass symbol on the lawn far below.

GOOD **EATS**

■ **AUGIE'S MUSSEL HOUSE**
Belgian-inspired dishes, including creative mussels offerings paired with ales. **1106 King St., tel 703-721-3970, $$$**

■ **BILBO BAGGINS GLOBAL RESTAURANT**
An American menu in a family-owned, casual setting. **208 Queen St., Alexandria, tel 703-683-0300, $$**

■ **THE FISH MARKET**
Chesapeake-style seafood in a historic warehouse. **105 King St., Alexandria, tel 703-836-5676, $$**

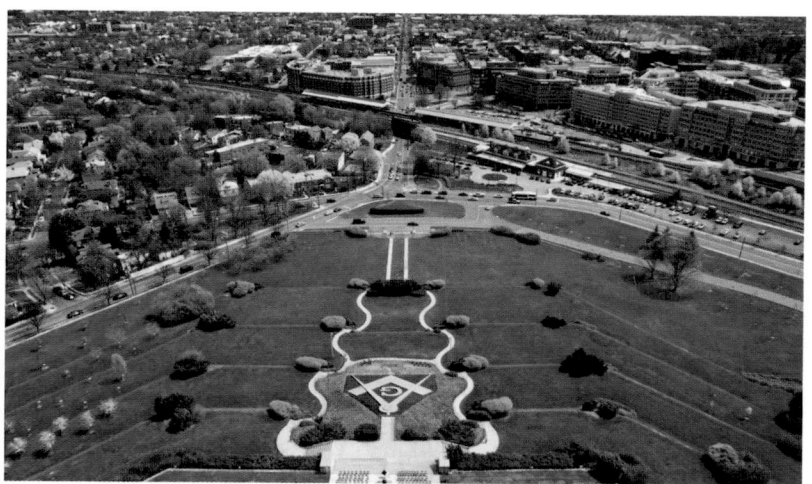

The view from the George Washington Masonic National Memorial

As you stroll back down King Street, make a detour south on Payne Street to Duke Street and the illuminating **Freedom House Museum** (*1315 Duke St., tel 703-746-4702, closed weekends*), which once held the nation's largest slave-trading business. Exhibits by the Northern Virginia Urban League remember the thousands who passed through—including Solomon Northrup, known for his memoir *Twelve Years A Slave*. If you don't want to walk the mile-plus (2 km) to the memorial from Washington Street, it's an easy drive; or you can hop aboard the free King Street Trolley, which runs every 10 minutes between the King Street–Old Town Metro station and Union Street.

101 Callahan Dr., Alexandria • tel 703-683-2007 • gwmemorial.org • tours daily at 9:30 a.m., 11 a.m., 1 p.m., 2:30 p.m., & 4 p.m. • $$$ • Metro: King St.–Old Town

Lyceum, Alexandria's History Museum

7 Take a stroll through Alexandria's past in this small museum, with exhibits telling the story of the city's original Native American settlements, its days as a colonial powerhouse and one of America's busiest ports, and the Civil War period in which it became the longest surrendered Confederate city (when the building itself served as a hospital). Artifacts, old photographs, maps, and original artwork add to the experience. A group of local Alexandrians founded the Lyceum in 1838 as an educational and cultural center.

201 S. Washington St. • tel 703-746-4994 • alexandriava.gov • $
• Metro: King St.–Old Town

Stabler-Leadbeater Apothecary Museum

8 George Washington, James Monroe, and Robert E. Lee all knew this family-run pharmacy, which operated between 1792 and 1933 and offered everything from tinctures to elixirs to cleaning products to paints to groceries. During the Civil War, when Alexandria was occupied by Union troops, soldiers stood in line here to purchase "hot drops," a cough medication containing paprika and alcohol. Preserved intact, the shop contains original potions, herbs, mortars, and journals. Look for the plaque showing the exact spot

Potions and powders from the Stabler-Leadbeater Apothecary kept generations healthy.

where Robert E. Lee was standing when he received the orders to put down the uprising at Harper's Ferry. Upstairs, the dark and musky, Harry Potter–esque manufacturing room, complete with wooden drawers labeled with such curious ingredients as Dragon's Blood and Gum Gambir, is where medicines were mixed and crushed. Visits by guided tour.

105–107 S. Fairfax St., Alexandria • tel 703-746-3852 • apothecarymuseum.org • by guided tour only; closed Mon.–Tues. Nov.–March • $$ • Metro: King St.–Old Town

SAVVY **TRAVELER**

George Washington lived (and died) at **Mount Vernon** (mountvernon.org), a plantation about 10 miles (16 km) south of Alexandria. Today it offers a fascinating glimpse into the life and times of the first president, with exhibits, tours of his home, gardens, and farm, plus breathtaking views over the Potomac. If you don't have a car, you can travel by boat cruise (potomacriverboatco.com). Another option is to bike to the estate along the riverside Mount Vernon Trail, then take a boat back to Alexandria (bikeandrolldc.com).

Torpedo Factory Art Center

9 Situated along the Potomac River, this former factory—yes, it actually made torpedoes—now contains 80-odd studios where you can watch local artists sculpt, paint, weave, and make stained glass (and buy their wares). Built in 1918, the factory turned out torpedo shell casings and other weaponry for both World Wars (look for the Mark XIV torpedo on view in the main hall, produced here in 1945). The federal government used the spacious building for storage until the city bought it in 1969. The art center opened in 1974, and it was incorporated into a waterfront development a decade later. The **Alexandria Archaeology Museum** on the third floor displays local artifacts (tel 703-746-4399, alexandriava.gov, closed Mon.).

Out back, amble along the boat docks, enjoy a meal at a nearby restaurant, or park yourself on a bench and take in the fresh air, along with musicians and other entertainers. Here, too, you can pick up a **water taxi** to the National Harbor development across the river, to a Nationals baseball game, or for a spin around the monuments, among other options (potomacriverboatco.com).

105 N. Union St., Alexandria • tel 703-746-4570 • torpedofactory.org • Metro: King St.–Old Town

OLD TOWN ALEXANDRIA

Christ Church

Many of America's forefathers worshipped at this colonial-era church.

The serene sanctuary of Christ Church; the wineglass pulpit dates from an 1890s restoration.

Built in the style of an English country church before the city of Alexandria was even established, Christ Church remains a bucolic oasis—and an active church—in the heart of the bustling city. Designed by James Wren and completed in 1773, it features a brick exterior and whitewashed interior. Its greatest claim to fame, however, is the fact that George Washington worshipped here, as did Robert E. Lee. Docents lead tours daily; meet at the church's front door.

■ MAIN CHURCH

Entering this bright space, you are immediately drawn in by the Palladian chancel window in front, unusual for its time. Note the cut-glass chandelier under the west gallery, advanced lighting in the early 1800s. George Washington was one of the first to purchase a box pew, now marked by a silver plaque (**No. 60**). The story goes that it was on the church's lawn that he declared his intent to fight the Revolutionary War. Robert E. Lee attended services here with his family from the age of three; a silver plaque on the chancel commemorates his confirmation here in 1853.

■ CHURCHYARD

Many of Alexandria's earliest residents were buried in the churchyard. By 1809, however, most burials were banned for sanitation and space concerns. Take a stroll around, reading the faint tombstones (although the gravestones that exist today are originals, they're not necessarily placed on their original spots; during the Civil War, Union soldiers stacked them against the Parish House and all order was

SAVVY **TRAVELER**

Old Town is filled with other early American churches, including:

Alfred Street Baptist Church (301 S. Alfred St.) Founded by slaves in 1803.

Old Presbyterian Meeting House (316 S. Royal St.) Dating from 1774.

St. Mary Catholic Church (310 S. Royal St.) Virginia's oldest Catholic church, founded in 1775.

St. Paul's Episcopal Church (228 S. Pitt St.) Benjamin Latrobe's only surviving Gothic Revival–style structure, dating from 1817.

lost). Among those laid to rest here are the city founder, Lord Mayor William Ramsay, and his wife, as well as Col. Philip Marsteller, one of George Washington's pallbearers (though his table stone monument was carted off during the Civil War). An unpretentious ivy-covered mound near Washington Street is the final resting place for Confederate prisoners of war.

■ MUSEUM

The **Memorial Parish House** maintains a small historic display, where plaques reveal more history about the church and its people through the centuries.

OLD TOWN ALEXANDRIA

118 N. Washington St., Alexandria • tel 703-549-1450 • historicchristchurch.org • Metro: King St.– Old Town

Colonial Alexandria

In the 18th century, Alexandria thrived as a key port city in the colony of Virginia. Against a backdrop of early settlement and revolutionary turmoil, daily life went on in taverns, riverfront businesses, and churches—with much debate about the growing British "situation." Today much of the colonial essence remains in brick and clapboard town houses, cobbled streets, and pocket gardens, while house museums give a sense of life at the start of America. Some typical characteristics:

OLD TOWN ALEXANDRIA

Above: Block after block of unbroken rows of narrow houses, their front doors opening to the street, add to Old Town Alexandria's charm. Opposite: Carlyle House, built in 1752, hosts many special events recalling the colonial era.

Architecture

Alexandria's earliest houses were built in the symmetrical Georgian style, with its classic proportions and ornamental elements. Beginning around 1780, the most prevalent style of architecture found here was named after its era, the federal period, and featured plainer surfaces and isolated detail.

Decor

The colonial-era elite looked to Europe for their furnishings and adornments, including hand-printed wallpaper, finely woven rugs, and ornate wood furniture made by skilled craftsmen. Those who couldn't afford such extravagance cobbled together what they could—homespun fabrics for curtains; braided, hand-woven, or hooked rugs; furniture made by local villagers, or the homeowners themselves. Common themes included the pineapple (symbol for hospitality), weeping willow (longevity), heart (love), and anchor (hope). Patterns such as stripes, plaids, and checks were also common.

Gardens

At a time when England was turning toward natural-istic gardens, the American colonists preferred the more conservative Anglo Dutch style—geometric symmetry within an enclosed space. Gardens, nor-mally planted behind the house in the urban centers due to space constraints, served to provide produce for the table, as well as beauty pleasing to the eye.

Churches

Church steeples spangled the colonial-era skyline. The Anglican church, or Church of England, was the established religion of Virginia, and Sunday services provided a social outlet. Attendance and taxes were mandatory by law. Little by little, other religions took hold, including Presbyterians, Methodists, Baptists, and Quakers—adding fuel to the fire of revolution, in a young land yearning for personal freedoms.

EARLY **HOMES**

Old Town Alexandria, along with Georgetown, is filled with edifices built at the time of the Revolutionary War. Some buildings are open to visitors as museums, others remain private. All provide a glimpse back into the nation's earliest days.

Captain's Row (late 18th c) Prince St. bet. S. Fairfax St. & S. Lee St., Alexandria, VA

Carlyle House (1752) 121 N. Fairfax St., Alexandria, VA

Old Stone House (1765) 3051 M St., N.W., Georgetown

Ramsay House (1724) 221 King St., Alexandria, VA

River Farm (1757) 7931 E. Boulevard Dr., Alexandria, VA

OLD TOWN ALEXANDRIA

Living History

Meet George Washington himself at Mount Vernon—then speak to a tenant farmer at a nearby farm to learn what life was like for other colonial-era Virginians. (Hint: They did not all live in multiroom mansions.) The greater Washington area is full of historic sights offering a chance to interact with historical figures—soldiers, doctors, farmers, innkeepers, and more—and experience where and how they lived. Here are some of the best.

OLD TOWN ALEXANDRIA

■ GADSBY'S TAVERN MUSEUM

Take tea with Martha Washington at the annual Ladies Tea, or join Gen. George Washington at the annual **Birthnight Banquet and Ball,** set in the year 1799 (period attire optional). Costumed interpreters lead daily tours and an after-hours candlelight tour.

134 N. Royal St., Alexandria • tel 703-746-4242 • gadsbystavern.org • $$–$$$$$ • Metro: King St.– Old Town

■ STABLER-LEADBEATER APOTHECARY MUSEUM

Watch reenactors conduct authentic 18th-century scientific experiments in this historic apothecary in Old Town Alexandria.

105–107 S. Fairfax St., Alexandria • tel 703-746-3852 • apothecarymuseum.org • by guided tour only; closed Mon.–Tues. Nov.–March • $$ • Metro: King St.– Old Town

■ CARLYLE HOUSE HISTORIC PARK

Meet members of the First Virginia Regiment at the **Annual Soldier's Christmas Open House Event,** just one of various reenactments that take place throughout the year at this historic manse in the heart of Old Town Alexandria. **John Carlyle's 1780 Funeral Reenactment** is another popular event.

121 N. Fairfax St., Alexandria • tel 703-549-2997 • nvrpa.org • $ • closed Mon. • Metro: King St.– Old Town

■ MOUNT VERNON

George Washington considered himself a farmer first and foremost, and, when he wasn't fighting wars or running the country, he devoted himself to improving American agriculture at his Mount Vernon plantation, about 10 miles (16 km) south of Alexandria.

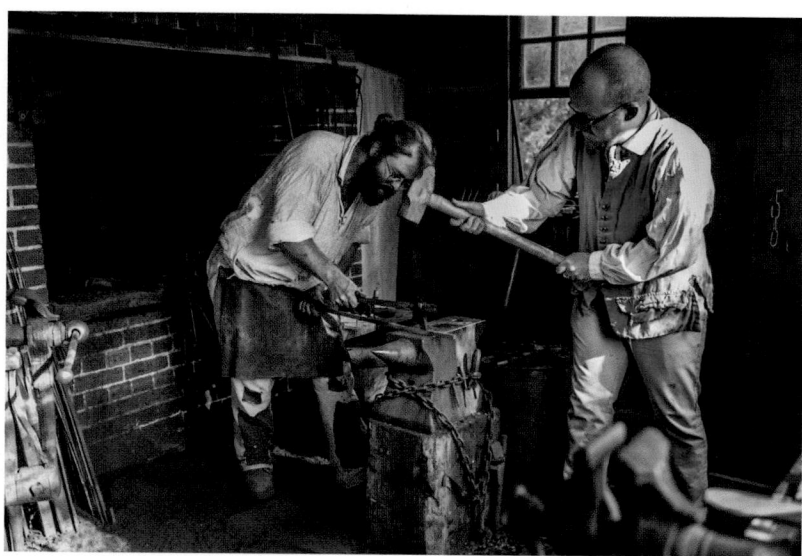

At Mount Vernon, tradesmen use tools and techniques common in colonial times.

Today, watch costumed interpreters demonstrate 18th-century agricultural methods and discuss events and issues of the day at the 16-sided treading barn (invented by Washington), slave cabin, and pole shelter. Other special events throughout the year include **Washington's birthday** (attended by the great general himself) and **Christmas at Mount Vernon,** when the plantation is decked out with colonial trimmings.

3200 Mount Vernon Memorial Highway, Mount Vernon • tel 703-780-2000 • mountvernon.org • $$$$ • Metro: Huntington, then Fairfax Connector Bus #101; see sidebar p. 169.

■ FORT WARD MUSEUM & HISTORIC SITE

Civil War–era soldiers and civilians reenact military life at this former Union Army installation built to defend Washington, D.C., during the Civil War—including infantry drills, artillery, camp life, and more. You'll talk firsthand to such famous people as Walt Whitman and Clara Barton, as well as surgeons, laundresses, engineers, and others.

4301 West Braddock Rd., Alexandria • tel 703-746-4848 • closed Mon. • alexandriava.gov • Metro: King St.–Old Town, then AT5 DASH bus to Landmark

Court of Neptune Fountain,
Library of Congress

PART 3

Travel Essentials

PLANNING YOUR TRIP

When to Go

April to May and September to November are the loveliest times to visit Washington, with generally comfortable temperatures and spectacular foliage—whether it's colorful blossoms or changing leaves. The busy tourism season starts in April with families and students on spring break. The cherry blossoms typically bloom around the Tidal Basin in late March or early April (see pp. 64–65); don't be surprised if it's still chilly at this time. July and August are hot and steamy, though many museums blast their air conditioners enough to warrant a light jacket. Winter is the low season, with modest snowstorms and freezing temperatures; when it does snow, streets may not be cleared immediately.

Rain is fairly evenly divided throughout the year (an average of 3.31 inches (8.4 cm) per month), except for afternoon thundershowers in June, July, and August.

What to Bring

Dress for the season and keep an umbrella handy. Heavy winter coats are usually essential December through February, and bring a light coat or jacket for the cooler spring or fall months (and even in summer for those air-conditioned museums). A hat in summer can help ward off the sun. Comfortable walking shoes are a given year-round.

VISITOR INFORMATION

The best source of visitor information is Destination D.C. (*washington.org*), Washington's official tourism site. It publishes a free visitors guide twice a year with comprehensive listings of attractions and events. Order or download it online.

NEGOTIATING THE CITY

When seeking a sight, first check the quadrant address, which indicates where it lies vis-à-vis the Capitol. Are you looking for N.W., N.E., S.W., or S.E.? The city is laid out in these four quadrants (see sidebar p. 9), with the Capitol building in the center. North Capitol, South Capitol, and East Capitol Streets radiate from this nucleus, separating the quadrants (the Mall runs west from the Capitol building).

Be advised that many District addresses can be found in more than one quadrant (for instance, there can be a 4000 M St. in N.E., S.E., S.W., and N.W.—four different D.C. locations).

After locating the quadrant, note that there are three types of streets in Washington. First are the numbered streets, running in a north–south direction from the Capitol. First Street, for instance, is located one block east or west of North or South Capitol Street, respectively.

The second street type is the lettered or named streets laid out in an east–west

direction. Starting from East Capitol Street or the Mall, the streets run through the alphabet (with the exceptions of J, X, Y, and Z). The ones nearest the Capitol are one-syllable words; when the alphabet has been run through, they become two syllables, then three. As such, you can tell how far a certain street is from the Capitol by the letter with which it begins and how many syllables it contains.

Finally, the avenues that are named after states run diagonally across the grid.

SECURITY

Security has become a major issue in many places worldwide, but it is especially a concern in and around Washington's public areas and government buildings. Streets are sometimes closed down with or without notice, and may be blocked off by concrete barriers.

Metal detectors are standard equipment in most public buildings. Be prepared to have your belongings scanned and searched. If you have a pacemaker or other medical device that might be affected, let the guards know. And do not carry anything that could be considered a weapon and might be confiscated—for example, Grandpa's treasured pocketknife.

The Washington D.C. Visitors Bureau has information on security measures and evacuation routes on its website (*washington.org*).

HOW TO GET TO WASHINGTON, D.C.

By Airplane

Washington, D.C., is served by three major airports: The closest is Ronald Reagan Washington National Airport (DCA) in Virginia, about 4 miles (6 km) from the city center; Washington Dulles International Airport (IAD), is 25 miles (40 km) west of Washington; and Baltimore–Washington International Thurgood Marshall Airport (BWI) stretches 25 miles (40 km) northeast of Washington, in Maryland.

DCA (known locally as "Reagan" or "National") is the closest airport to the city and also the most convenient. Washington's Metro system has a station right there. Taxi fare downtown is about $20. IAD (called "Dulles") is served by its own Washington Flyer taxi fleet (tel 703-572-8294, washfly.com), with 24-hour service to and from the airport. Taxi fare to downtown Washington from Dulles is about $60. Washington Flyer also operates coach service (tel 703-572-7661) connecting Dulles to the Wiehle–Reston East Metro station for about $5 one way. A Dulles Airport Metro extension and station are under construction and expected to open in 2021.

The best way to get to and from BWI Airport is by train. Both MARC's Penn Line (tel 866-743-3682, weekdays only) and Amtrak (tel 800-872-7245, must buy ticket for specific train) provide frequent service between Union Station on Capitol Hill and BWI's own rail station; a free shuttlebus connects the rail station and the airport terminal. Taxis between BWI and downtown D.C. cost about $90.

Airport Information

For general airport information: Reagan National (tel 703-417-8000), Dulles (tel 703-572-2700), and BWI (tel 410-859-7111, bwiairport.com); Dulles and Reagan share a website (metwashairports.com).

By Train

Amtrak trains arrive at Washington's Union Station on Capitol Hill (see p. 72). Although locals use the train mostly as a fast, convenient way to get to New York on the Acela and Northeast Regional trains, Washington is a major rail hub, connecting the capital by train to most U.S. destinations with rail service. The Metro station at Union Station provides easy access to the rest of the city and beyond.

Amtrak information: tel 800-872-7245, amtrak.com

GETTING AROUND

By Metro

The Washington Metropolitan Area Transit Authority operates the bus and subway systems in the metropolitan area. Metrorail stations are clearly marked by large columns with brown "M" signs.

The clean and efficient rail network makes it very easy to get around the region, but maintenance and repairs required from the growing number of riders means there may be occasional delays or outages on some sections of the system. In such cases bus transfer between stations is usually available. Metro posts regular updates about operating status (wmata.com). Most suburban stations have lots for all-day parking, but go early because they fill up fast.

Fares range from roughly $1.85 to $6.00 one way, based on distance and time of day. You must purchase a plastic, rechargeable SmarTrip card, available online, at any Metrorail station, at CVS pharmacies in the D.C. area, and at other retail outlets. Fare information is available near the ticket machines.

Metrorail opens at 5 a.m. on weekdays and 7 a.m. on weekends. It closes at midnight Sunday through Thursday. On Friday and Saturday nights, it runs until 3 a.m.

Metro route information: tel 202-637-7000, wmata.com

By Bus

Metrobus service covers the city and the suburbs, with some lines running 24 hours. The fare for any destination within Washington is $2, or $4.25 for express service. Exact fare is required. For route and fare information, tel 202-637-7000, wmata.com. For just $1 per ride, the DC Circulator bus service operates daily in central Washington, with frequent stops. The five routes extend from Dupont Circle to Rosslyn; Georgetown to Union Station; Union Station to Navy Yard; Woodley Park to McPherson Square; Potomac Avenue to Skyland; and around the National Mall. Visit *dccirculator.com* for route schedules and maps.

By Taxi
Cabs in Washington are plentiful and fairly inexpensive. It's usually possible to hail a cab on any major street. They run on a meter system, and there are surcharges for each extra passenger, rush hour, snow emergency, and baggage. Information on surcharges is posted in every cab.

By Bicycle
The popular bike-sharing program, Capital Bikeshare (*capitalbikeshare.com*), offers more than 5,000 bikes at more than 500 stations throughout the District as well as in nearby Arlington, Virginia; Alexandria, Virginia; and Montgomery County, Maryland. The distinctive bright-red bikes can be found at most Metro stations and at convenient locations downtown and along the National Mall. Regular users can buy a daily, monthly, or annual membership online, while visitors can use a credit card at any Bikeshare station kiosk to purchase a 24-hour pass for $8.00 or a 3-day pass for $17. You can also rent a bike hourly (from $2 first hour). Note that bike helmets, required by law for riders under age 16, are not available.

By Car
Visitors should consider the possibility that a car will be more of an annoyance than a convenience. Parking is difficult, and parking garages are expensive.

Should you find on-street parking, check the signs, since many streets become no-parking zones during rush hour. If your car is not where you left it, call *tel 202-541-6083* for information on its location.

Some streets are two-way most of the time, but during rush hour become one way— including Rock Creek and Potomac Parkways and 17th Street, N.W.

TRAVELERS WITH DISABILITIES
D.C. is a very accessible place for travelers with disabilities. The Washington Metropolitan Area Transit Authority also publishes a free pamphlet on Metro's bus and rail system accessibility for the elderly and physically disabled. Call *tel 202-962-1100* to order the guide, or visit Metro's website at *wmata.com*.

Smithsonian museum buildings are accessible to wheelchair visitors. Find detailed information online at *si.edu* or call *tel 202-633-2921*.

Government buildings are generally open to the public, but be advised that they may close for security reasons with little or no notice. Be flexible, and call ahead.

CRIME & EMERGENCIES
Crimes of all sorts have been on the decrease in the last few years in Washington, but precautions are advised.

Don't wander onto deserted or ill-lighted streets or parks, particularly at night. If you're uncomfortable in a neighborhood, leave.

If someone tries to rob you, give the robber whatever he or she asks. Remember, your life is more valuable than your belongings.

Emergency Numbers
In an emergency, call 911.

- Police/fire/ambulance: 911

- City Services and information (non-emergency): 311

- Metro Transit Police (emergency): 202-962-2121

- International Visitors Information Desk (offers multilingual information and assistance; located at Dulles): 703-572-2536

- Travelers Aid: 202-371-1937

- U.S. Park Police (emergency): 202-610-7500

Lost Credit Cards
American Express: 800-528-4800

Diners Club: 800-234-6377
Discover Card: 800-347-2683
MasterCard: 800-424-7787
Visa: 800-847-2911

TRAVEL ESSENTIALS

HOTELS

When it comes to travel, where you sleep can make all the difference. Washington, a city that host guests from all nations, offers a panoply of selections in all price categories and styles.

Washington hotels vary from the luxurious and very expensive—the Four Seasons in Georgetown and the Mandarin Oriental near the National Mall included—to the basic and still fairly expensive, such as the large downtown hotels that cater mostly to the convention and meeting trade. Small and charming is harder to find, but the new boutique hotels opened by the Kimpton Group are a hopeful sign.

Because every business in the country is affected by government legislation and regulations, Washington hotels are flooded by business travelers on expense accounts. That means high prices during the week, when businesses are paying the tab, with weekend bargains for leisure and family travelers.

Hotels in the city are expensive, so some visitors prefer to stay in less expensive places in suburban Virginia or Maryland and travel into the city each day. Many hotels routinely offer rates cheaper than their posted rack rates, and many properties offer discounts through organizations such as AAA or AARP. Note that most are nonsmoking establishments.

Organization
Hotels are listed by chapter area, then by price category, then alphabetically. Hotel restaurants

of note are also included.

Price Range
An indication of the cost of a double room in the high season is given by **$** signs.
$$$$$	Over $225
$$$$	$175–$225
$$$	$125–$175
$$	$85–$125
$	Under $85

Text Symbols
- 🛏 *No. of Guest Rooms*
- 🅿 *Parking*
- ⬍ *Elevator*
- 🏊 *Outdoor Pool*
- 🏊 *Indoor Pool*
- 🏋 *Gym*
- 📶 *Wi-Fi*
- 💳 *Credit Cards*
- Ⓜ *Metro*

NATIONAL MALL

■ MANDARIN ORIENTAL
$$$$$
1330 MARYLAND AVE., S.W.
TEL 202-554-8588
mandarinoriental.com/washington

This super-luxury hotel near the National Mall's southeastern end overlooks the Tidal Basin and the Jefferson Memorial. The marble baths, lacquered furniture, silk furnishings, and extensive spa services make for a soothing stay.

🛏 *400* 🅿 🏊 🏋 📶 *Free* 💳 *All major cards* Ⓜ *L'Enfant Plaza*

CAPITOL HILL

■ THE GEORGE
$$$$$
15 E ST., N.W.
TEL 202-347-4200 OR 800-576-8331
hotelgeorge.com

A completely renovated building (from 1928), the George is a Kimpton hotel with striking decor, convenient to Capitol Hill attractions. The restaurant **Bistro Bis** *(tel 202-661-2700)* offers quality contemporary French bistro fare.

🛏 *139* 🅿 🅿 📶 *Charge* 💳 *All major cards* Ⓜ *Union Station*

■ CAPITOL HILL HOTEL
$$$$
200 C ST., S.E.
TEL 202-543-6000
capitolhillhotel-dc.com

Tucked behind the Library of Congress on the House side of the Hill, this hotel offers kitchenettes in every room and suite.

🛏 *153* 🅿 📶 *Free* 💳 *All major cards* Ⓜ *Capitol South*

■ CAPITOL SKYLINE HOTEL
$$$$
10 I ST., S.W.
202-488-7500 OR 800-458-7500
capitolskyline.com

With a free shuttle to D.C.'s major sites, this seven-story downtown hotel is a celebration of modern design: The building itself is the masterwork of Morris Lapidus of

TRAVEL ESSENTIALS

Miami Beach fame, with furniture in the lobby by the likes of Frank Gehry, Eero Saarinen, and Philippe Starck. The decor of the large and light-filled guest rooms is a modern take on colonial style. While the hotel is perfectly safe, it is not necessarily advisable to walk in the surrounding neighborhood after dark.
🛈 203 🅿 $ 🍽 ♿ 📺 📶 *Free* 💳 *All major cards* Ⓜ *Navy Yard–Ballpark*

■ COURTYARD WASHINGTON CAPITOL HILL/NAVY YARD

$$$$
140 L ST., S.E.
TEL 202-479-0027
marriott.com
A friendly staff and airy suites with refrigerators, microwaves, and wet bars add to the allure of this modern hotel located near a thriving neighborhood full of restaurants and bars—and a baseball's toss from Nationals Park—with a Metro nearby.
🛈 192 + 12 suites 🅿 *Valet* 🍽 ♿ 📺 📶 *Free* 💳 *All major cards* Ⓜ *Navy Yard–Ballpark*

■ HYATT REGENCY WASHINGTON ON CAPITOL HILL

$$$$
400 NEW JERSEY AVE., N.W.
TEL 202-737-1234 OR 800-223-1234
hyatt.com
This large convention hotel with all the amenities occupies a full city block on Capitol Hill. Museums, monuments, and more are just steps away.
🛈 838 🅿 ♿ 📺 📶 *Free* 💳 *All major cards* Ⓜ *Union Station*

■ LIAISON CAPITOL HILL HOTEL

$$$$
415 NEW JERSEY AVE., N.W.
TEL 202-638-1616
yotel.com
This boutique hotel, located between Union Station and Capitol Hill, features a rooftop bar, seasonal pool, and the **Art and Soul** restaurant *(tel 202-393-7777).*
🛈 343 ♿ 📺 📶 *Free* 💳 *All major cards* Ⓜ *Union Station*

■ PHOENIX PARK HOTEL

$$$$
520 N. CAPITOL ST., N.W.
TEL 202-638-6900 OR 855-371-6824
phoenixparkhotel.com
Named after a park in Dublin, this hotel has a European ambience. The adjoining **Dubliner Restaurant and Pub** *(tel 202-737-3773)* offers good pub cooking and Irish entertainment.
🛈 149 🅿 📺 📶 *Free* 💳 *All major cards* Ⓜ *Union Station*

■ WASHINGTON COURT HOTEL

$$$$
525 NEW JERSEY AVE., N.W.
TEL 202-628-2100
washingtoncourthotel.com
This convenient, comfortable hotel has a dramatic four-story atrium lobby and billiards in the Federal City bar.
🛈 265 🅿 📺 📶 *Free in public areas* 💳 *All major cards* Ⓜ *Union Station*

WHITE HOUSE & AROUND

■ FAIRMONT HOTEL

$$$$$
2401 M ST., N.W.
TEL 202-429-2400 OR 800-257-7544
fairmont.com/washington
Built around a courtyard, the Fairmont is in the West End area of town near Georgetown. Rooms are luxurious, service is attentive. The fitness center, with pool, is one of the city's most popular. **Juniper** *(tel 202-457-5020)* offers modern American regional cooking.
🛈 413 🅿 ♿ 📺 📶 *Free in public areas* 💳 *All major cards* Ⓜ *Foggy Bottom–GWU*

■ THE HAY–ADAMS HOTEL

$$$$$
800 16TH ST., N.W.
TEL 202-638-6600 OR 800-853-6807
hayadams.com
Built where President Lincoln's secretary John Hay and John Adams's grandson Henry Adams lived, the hotel is just across Lafayette Square from the White House. **The Lafayette** dining room *(tel 202-638-2570)* and guest rooms on the south side offer great views.
🛈 145 🅿 📶 *Free* 💳 *All major cards* Ⓜ *Farragut West, McPherson Square*

■ THE JEFFERSON

$$$$$
1200 16TH ST., N.W.
TEL 202-448-2300
jeffersondc.com
Regarded by many as the Capital City's finest small hotel, the Jefferson showcases many

touches inspired by the third president of the United States.
[i] 99 [P] 📶 *Free* 🅰 *All major cards* 🅿 *Farragut West and North*

■ PARK HYATT
$$$$$
1201 24TH ST., N.W.
TEL 202-789-1234
parkwashington.hyatt.com
Three blocks from Georgetown, in D.C.'s West End, the Park Hyatt has a lobby decorated with an impressive collection of art plus large and luxurious rooms. Its **Blue Duck Tavern** *(tel 202-419-6755)* serves accomplished meals including a lavish weekend brunch.
[i] 220 [P] 🍴 📶 *Free* 🅰 *All major cards* 🅿 *Foggy Bottom–GWU*

■ RENAISSANCE MAYFLOWER HOTEL
$$$$$
1127 CONNECTICUT AVE., N.W.
TEL 202-347-3000 OR
800-228-7697
themayflowerhotel.com
Once home to many members of Congress, this stylish hotel has been the site of many inaugural balls. The gracious lobby runs an entire city block.
[i] 581 [P] 🍴 📶 *Free in public areas* 🅰 *All major cards* 🅿 *Farragut North*

■ SOFITEL LAFAYETTE SQUARE
$$$$
806 15TH ST., N.W.
TEL 202-730-8800
sofitel-washington-dc.com
Set in an 1880s building near the White House, this hotel has a restrained elegance. Its restaurant, **Opaline Bar &
Brasserie** *(tel 202-730-8700),*

serves French cuisine and also has a popular bar with patio.
[i] 237 [P] 🍴 📶 *Free* 🅰 *All major cards* 🅿 *McPherson Square*

■ THE ST. REGIS
$$$$$
923 16TH ST., N.W.
TEL 202-638-2626 OR
888-627-8087
stregiswashingtondc.com
The posh St. Regis, located near the White House and museums, boasts fine plasterwork ceilings, antiques, and ornate chandeliers.
[i] 172 [P] 🍴 📶 *Free* 🅰 *All major cards* 🅿 *Farragut North*

■ WILLARD INTERCONTINENTAL
$$$$$
1401 PENNSYLVANIA AVE., N.W.
TEL 202-628-9100 OR
800-424-6835
washington.intercontinental
.com
A Willard hotel has been on this site since 1850. Abraham Lincoln stayed here before his inauguration, and Julia Ward Howe wrote "The Battle Hymn of the Republic" here. The hotel has recently been luxuriously updated. Its **Café du Parc** *(tel 202-942-7000)* features French bistro cuisine and exquisite pastries.
[i] 335 [P] 🍴 📶 *Charge* 🅰 *All major cards* 🅿 *Metro Center*

■ W WASHINGTON D.C.
$$$$
515 15TH ST., N.W.
TEL 202-661-2400
wwashingtondc.com
Italian Renaissance meets modern cool in this beautifully refurbished hotel boasting a

Bliss spa and the rooftop **POV** bar *(tel 202-661-2400),* with its fabulous views of D.C.
[i] 326 📶 *Free* 🅰 *All major cards* 🅿 *Metro Center*

■ ARC THE.HOTEL
$$$–$$$$
824 NEW HAMPSHIRE AVE., N.W.
TEL 202-337-6620 OR
800-426-4455
arcthehoteldc.com
This vintage hotel, with Georgetown and the National Mall within walking distance, has been totally revamped in chic modern style and with the hip **Notti 824** *(tel 202-298-8085)* cocktail bar.
[i] 136 [P] *Valet* 🔌 🍴 📶 *Free* 🅰 *All major cards* 🅿 *Foggy Bottom–GWU*

■ HOTEL LOMBARDY
$$$
2019 PENNSYLVANIA AVE., N.W.
TEL 202-828-2600
hotellombardy.com
Conveniently located near the White House and the National Mall, this romantic boutique hotel occupies a 1926 art deco apartment building decorated with European antiques. Some guest rooms have a separate sitting area and wet bar.
[i] 140 [P] 🔌 🍴 📶 *Free* 🅰 *All major cards* 🅿 *Foggy Bottom–GWU*

DOWNTOWN

■ THE HAMILTON CROWNE PLAZA
$$$$$
1001 14TH ST., N.W.
TEL 202-682-0111 OR
66-407-1764
hamiltonhoteldc.com

This small art deco hotel offers guests an elegant lobby and small, rich-colored rooms with modern amenities. Its location in the heart of the business district, near the White House as well as the National Mall, can't be beat.
🛈 *318 rooms + 17 suites* 🅿 *$*
🛗 🍴 🛜 *Free* 🅐 *All major cards*
Ⓜ *McPherson Square*

■ HOTEL MONACO
$$$$$
700 F ST., N.W.
TEL 202-628-7177 OR
855-546-7866
monaco-dc.com
This luxury Kimpton boutique hotel is housed in the stately 1839 Tariff Building in Penn Quarter, within steps of the action of the Verizon Center, Washington Convention Center, and 7th Street arts scene. Distinctive rooms with 15-foot (5 m) ceilings feature neoclassical furnishings and vivid colors.
🛈 *184* 🅿 🍴 🛜 *Charge* 🅐 *All major cards* Ⓜ *Gallery Place–Chinatown*

■ HOTEL ZENA
$$$$–$$$$$
1155 14TH ST., N.W.
TEL 202-737-1200
donovanhousehotel.com
A rooftop pool and bar, pod-shaped spiral showers, a black-and-white with purple highlights color scheme, and complimentary wine hour highlight this recently revamped yet über-hip boutique hotel on Thompson Circle. Its sleek new edgy styling is now the chicest in town.
🛈 *191 + 17 suites* 🅿 *Valet*
🛗 🍴 🛜 🅐 *All major cards*
Ⓜ *McPherson Square, Mt. Vernon Sq 7th St–Convention Center*

■ HENLEY PARK HOTEL
$$$$
926 MASSACHUSETTS AVE., N.W.
TEL 202-638-5200 OR
800-222-8474
henleypark.com
A Tudor-style hotel in the tradition of Europe's finest inns is one of D.C.'s most charming. Dozens of gargoyles and lead windows grace its exterior.
🛈 *96* 🅿 🍴 🛜 *Free* 🅐 *All major cards* Ⓜ *Mount Vernon Sq 7th St–Convention Center, Gallery Place–Chinatown*

■ THE MADISON
$$$$
1177 15TH ST., N.W.
TEL 202-862-1600
3.hilton.com
Cozy and noted for its attentive service, The Madison offers a great location for exploring D.C. sights as well as the Dupont Circle area, being mere steps from the White House.
🛈 *356* 🅿 🍴 🛜 *Free* 🅐 *All major cards* Ⓜ *McPherson Square*

■ MORRISON-CLARK INN
$$$$
1011 L ST., N.W.
TEL 202-898-1200 OR
800-332-7898
morrisonclark.com
This stately Victorian inn just off Massachusetts Avenue was built as two townhomes in 1864. A grand expansion into the church next door doubled the room count. Chefs of the **Morrison-Clark Restaurant** (tel 202-989-1200) have won many awards for their New American cuisine.
🛈 *114* 🅿 🍴 🛜 *Free* 🅐 *All major cards* Ⓜ *Mount Vernon Sq 7th St–Convention Center*

■ HOTEL HARRINGTON
$$$
436 11TH ST., N.W.
TEL 202-628-8140 OR
800-424-8532
hotel-harrington.com
Low prices, a prime location, and very plain, clean rooms make the Hotel Harrington popular with school groups and others on a tight budget.
🛈 *242* 🛜 *Free* 🅐 *All major cards* Ⓜ *Metro Center*

DUPONT CIRCLE & ADAMS MORGAN

■ EMBASSY CIRCLE GUEST HOUSE
$$$$$
2224 R ST., N.W.
TEL 202-232-7744
embassycircleguesthouse.com
Tucked away on a tree-shaded street on Embassy Circle, this genteel B&B occupies the former Taiwanese embassy. Each room is individually decorated with antiques, original artwork, and Persian carpets. The complimentary breakfast is served in the formal dining room, and a wine hour is offered each evening. It's located just steps from Dupont Circle, with easy Metro access.
🛈 *9 suites* 🅿 *Valet* 🛗 🛜 *Free* 🅐 *All major cards* Ⓜ *Dupont Circle*

■ THE NORMANDY INN
$$$$$
2118 WYOMING AVE., N.W.
TEL 202-483-1350
thenormandydc.com
Though rooms are small, a cozy wine hour, free afternoon tea and coffee (and fresh-baked

cookies!), and attentive service entice guests to return time and again to this chic, European-style hotel. The small patio in back is charming. Located near Adams Morgan and Dupont Circle, with the major D.C. sights a short Metro hop away.

🛈 75 🅿 Valet 🔁 📺 📶 Free 🍽 All major cards 🚇 Dupont Circle

■ PALOMAR HOTEL

$$$$$

2121 P ST., N.W.
TEL 202-448-1800 OR
855-546-7866

hotelpalomar-dc.com

Sophistication and personalized service are the hallmarks of this Kimpton hotel inspired by 1930s French moderne style. Exotic woods, bold art, and geometric touches abound in this hotel, which has a gourmet diner restaurant.

🛈 335 🅿 ♿ 📺 📶 Free 🍽 All major cards 🚇 Dupont Circle

■ CHURCHILL HOTEL

$$$$

1914 CONNECTICUT AVE., N.W.
TEL 202-797-2000 OR
844-823-4697

thechurchillhotel.com

Located just north of the vibrant Dupont Circle area, the Churchill offers sophisticated 18th-century-themed contemporary styling.

🛈 173 🅿 📺 📶 Free 🍽 All major cards 🚇 Dupont Circle

■ THE DUPONT CIRCLE HOTEL

$$$$

1500 NEW HAMPSHIRE AVE., N.W.
TEL 202-483-6000

doylecollection.com

Overlooking Dupont Circle, this spacious, elegant boutique hotel includes a Presidential Suite and 9,000 feet (2,740 m)of meeting space. All rooms have mini bars and free bottled water.

🛈 327 🅿 📺 📶 Free 🍽 All major cards 🚇 Dupont Circle

■ THE FAIRFAX AT EMBASSY ROW

$$$$

2100 MASSACHUSETTS AVE., N.W.
TEL 202-293-2100 OR
855-559-8899

fairfaxwashingtondc.com

Formerly the Westin Embassy Row, the hotel dates from 1924 and has been for many years the residential hotel favored by members of Congress. Former Vice President Al Gore basically grew up here. Guest rooms are luxurious, as one would expect from a hotel on Massachusetts Avenue's Embassy Row.

🛈 259 🅿 📺 📶 Free in public areas 🍽 All major cards 🚇 Dupont Circle

■ HOTEL MADERA

$$$$

1310 NEW HAMPSHIRE AVE., N.W.
TEL 202-296-7600 OR
844-781-1152

hotelmadera.com

This pampering hideaway is like a sophisticated B&B tucked in a quiet location near downtown office buildings and embassies.

🛈 82 🅿 📶 Free 🍽 All major cards 🚇 Dupont Circle

■ THE LINE

$$$$

1770 EUCLID ST., N.W.
TEL 202-588-0525

thelinehotel.com/dc

On the edge of millennial-friendly Adams Morgan, this chic and artsy newcomer, housed in a converted neoclassical church, offers meticulously curated rooms furnished with pieces from local flea markets, plus a mini-library and original art. Great design, three gourmet restaurants, plus live music form a Holy Trinity to which guests say "Amen!"

🛈 197 rooms, 23 suites 🅿 📶 Free 🍽 All major cards 🚇 Dupont Circle

■ MASON & ROOK HOTEL

$$$$

1430 RHODE ISLAND AVE., N.W.
TEL 202-762-3100

masonandrookhotel.com

You'll feel as if you're visiting your urbanite friend's chic home at this boutique hotel—one with Frette linens, in-room yoga mats, and an evening wine hour. Boasting some of the city's largest guest rooms, it's located on a quiet road near trendy 14th Street.

🛈 178 🅿 Valet 🔁 ♿ 📺 📶 Charge 🍽 All major cards 🚇 Dupont Circle

■ OMNI SHOREHAM HOTEL

$$$$

2500 CALVERT ST., N.W.
TEL 202-234-0700

omnishorehamhotel.com

Opened in 1930 on 11 landscaped acres (4.4 ha) near Rock Creek Park—with its jogging trails and paths—the Shoreham has tastefully appointed rooms and is popular with conventions and large events.

🛈 834 📺 📶 Free in public areas 🍽 All major cards 🚇 Woodley Park–Zoo– Adams Morgan

■ ROUGE

$$$$
1315 16TH ST., N.W.
TEL 202-232-8000 OR
855-546-7866
rougehotel.com
A total revamp in 2020 infused exciting contemporary styling to this hip Kimpton hotel within walking distance of Dupont Circle.
🚹 144 🛎 📶 Free ⛷ All major cards 🚇 Dupont Circle, McPherson Square

■ SWANN HOUSE

$$$–$$$$$
1808 NEW HAMPSHIRE AVE., N.W.
TEL 202-265-4414
swannhouse.com
Occupying an 1833 Dupont Circle mansion, this homey inn features nine stylishly decorated guest rooms, each one with a different theme, from lighthouse to French country. A sip of sherry in the sitting room is an especially nice touch. Dupont Circle and Adams Morgan restaurants are within easy reach.

🚹 9 🅿️ 🏊 📶 Free ⛷ All major cards 🚇 Dupont Circle

■ TABARD INN

$$$
1739 N ST., N.W.
TEL 202-931-5197
tabardinn.com
This small hotel is beloved by those who consider it quaint and adore the Victorian clutter. Locals frequent the hotel's **restaurant** (tel 202-331-8528), which has a charming outdoor garden and imaginative food. The rooms vary widely in size, so look before you commit.

🚹 35 🅿️ 📶 Free ⛷ All major cards 🚇 Dupont Circle

■ KALORAMA GUEST HOUSE

$$
2700 CATHEDRAL AVE., N.W.
TEL 202-588-8188
kaloramaguesthouse.com
Located near the zoo, this Woodley Park guesthouse offers B&B-style accommodation in the European tradition. This means some shared baths, as well as continental breakfast, afternoon lemonade, and sherry in the evening. The many repeat customers can help attest to its comfortable atmosphere.
🚹 19 📶 Free ⛷ All major cards 🚇 Woodley Park–Zoo–Adams Morgan

GEORGETOWN

■ FOUR SEASONS HOTEL

$$$$$
2800 PENNSYLVANIA AVE., N.W.
TEL 202-342-0444
fourseasons.com/washington
Located on the very eastern edge of Georgetown, this luxurious hotel provides its guests with a civilized home base for the rest of the city. On site, the **Seasons** restaurant (tel 202-342-0444), overlooking the C & O Canal, is a favorite power breakfast spot. Also popular, the welcoming and well-appointed three-level fitness center with an adjoining spa is one of the most opulent in town.
🚹 222 🅿️ 🏊 🛎 📶 Free ⛷ All major cards 🚇 Foggy Bottom–GWU

■ THE GRAHAM GEORGETOWN

$$$$$
1075 THOMAS JEFFERSON ST., N.W.
TEL 202-337-0900
thegrahamgeorgetown.com
Named for one-time Georgetown neighborhood resident Alexander Graham Bell, this posh hotel includes such touches as pillow-top mattresses and l'Occitane bath amenities. It is located close to the historic C & O Canal and its scenic towpath. **The Rooftop** (tel 202-337-0900) rooftop bar and lounge offers panoramic views of the Washington skyline.
🚹 57 📶 Free ⛷ All major cards 🚇 Foggy Bottom–GWU

■ RITZ-CARLTON GEORGETOWN

$$$$$
3100 SOUTH ST., N.W.
TEL 202-912-4100
ritzcarlton.com
Built on the site of what was once a brick incinerator building, complete with a 130-foot-high (40 m) smokestack, this luxury hotel offers a soothing retreat overlooking the Potomac waterfront.
🚹 86 🅿️ 🛎 📶 Free in public areas ⛷ All major cards 🚇 Foggy Bottom–GWU

■ THE WESTIN GEORGETOWN, WASHINGTON D.C.

$$$$$
2350 M ST., N.W.
TEL 202-429-0100
westin.com/washingtondc
This low-key hotel, located between Georgetown and the

TRAVEL ESSENTIALS

White House, is known for its friendly, attentive service. Comfortable rooms and a great location offer good value for visitors to Washington.

🛈 248 🅿 Valet 🌄 📺 📶 Free in public areas 🔷 All major cards 🚇 Foggy Bottom–GWU

■ THE GEORGETOWN INN
$$$$
1310 WISCONSIN AVE., N.W.
TEL 202-333-8900

georgetowninn.com
This classic redbrick hotel has colonial decor, large rooms, and marble bathrooms. It's also conveniently located for Georgetown shopping and entertainment.

🛈 96 🅿 📺 📶 Free in public areas 🔷 All major cards 🚇 Foggy Bottom–GWU

OLD TOWN ALEXANDRIA

■ MORRISON HOUSE
$$$$$
116 S. ALFRED ST.
TEL 703-838-8000

morrisonhouse.com
Recently reopened after a multimillion-dollar renovation, this boutique hotel evokes the atmosphere of Old Alexandria. Guest rooms are tastefully furnished in federal-period reproductions. If your schedule allows, dinner and craft cocktails are offered at the hotel's acclaimed **The Study** (tel 703-838-8000) restaurant and bar, with live entertainment on site.

🛈 45 🅿 📶 Charge 🔷 All major cards 🚇 King Street–Old Town

■ THE ALEXANDRIAN
$$$
480 KING ST.
TEL 703-549-6080 OR
888-236-2427

thealexandrian.com
This centrally located, recently refurbished boutique hotel features lively and sophisticated decor. A hosted wine hour and fitness center are some of the extra touches that make it a favored destination.

🛈 241 📺 📺 📶 Charge 🔷 All major cards 🚇 King Street–Old Town

■ HAMPTON INN OLD TOWN
$$$
1616 KING ST.
TEL 703-299-9900

hamptoninn.com
Located in the heart of historic Old Town and near the Metro, this well-run hotel combines comfort and value with convenience. You can walk to many restaurants in the area.

🛈 80 📺 📺 📶 Free 🔷 All major cards 🚇 King Street–Old Town

■ HILTON ALEXANDRIA OLD TOWN
$$$
1767 KING ST.
TEL 703-837-0440 OR
800-445-8667

hilton.com
Just steps from the Metro, convenient to Alexandria's charming Old Town, this upscale hotel has clean, nicely appointed rooms.

🛈 241 🅿 📺 📺 📶 Free in public areas 🔷 All major cards 🚇 King Street–Old Town

ARLINGTON

■ RITZ-CARLTON PENTAGON CITY
$$$$$
1250 S. HAYES ST.
TEL 703-415-5000

ritzcarlton.com
Part of the Fashion Centre mall, this hotel offers luxury with the added advantage of shopping. Modern American cuisine and a popular afternoon tea are served in the **Fyve Restaurant Lounge** (tel 703-412-2762).

🛈 366 🅿 📺 📺 📶 Free in public areas 🔷 All major cards 🚇 Pentagon City

■ CRYSTAL CITY MARRIOTT
$$$$
1999 JEFFERSON DAVIS HWY.
TEL 703-413-5500

marriott.com
Located a mile (1.6 km) from Reagan National Airport, this hotel connects to the Crystal City Metro stop, offering easy access to the memorials and Smithsonian museums.

🛈 343 📺 📺 📶 Free in public areas 🔷 All major cards 🚇 Crystal City

■ KEY BRIDGE MARRIOTT
$$$$
1401 LEE HWY.
TEL 703-524-6400

marriott.com
Just across from Georgetown, this hotel has easy access by Metro to downtown sites. **Revival Restaurant** (tel 703-524-6400) offers casual dining and buffet breakfasts.

🛈 582 🌄 📺 📶 Free in public areas 🔷 All major cards 🚇 Rosslyn

INDEX

Boldface indicates illustrations.

A

Adams Memorial 125
Adams Morgan 128, **128,** 134–135, **135,** 140, 184–186
Adams Morgan Day 140
African American Civil War Memorial and Museum 35, 37
African-American heritage 34–37
Alexandria Visitor Center at Ramsay House 161, 162
Anacostia Community Museum 35, 37
Anderson House 129, **130,** 131–132
Arena Stage 22, 25, 100–101
Arlington, Virginia: hotels 187
Arlington National Cemetery 18, 21
Art Museum of the Americas & Organization of American States 109, 114–115, **115**

B

Barracks Row (Eighth Street) 69, 70, 77
Bars **5,** 25, 84–85, **85**
Belmont–Paul Women's Equality National Monument 71, **71,** 75
Biking 26, 28–29, 65
Boundary stones **82,** 83
Bus tours 17

C

Capitol Hill 68–85
  Barracks Row (Eighth Street) 69, 70, 77
  Belmont–Paul Women's Equality National Monument 71, **71,** 75
  capital city **82,** 82–83, **83**
  D.C. in a day 15, 17
  Eastern Market 23, **23,** 24, 69, 70, **70,** 76–77, **77**
  Emancipation Memorial 124
  Folger Shakespeare Library 71, 76
  hotels 181–182
  Library of Congress 17, 23, **23,** 24, 71, 72–73, **73**
  map 70–71
  restaurants 37, 75
  Union Station 70, **70,** 72
  U.S. Supreme Court 17, 23, 24, 71, **74,** 74–75
  watering holes 84–85, **85**
  see also U.S. Capitol
Capitol Steps (group) 27, 29
Carlyle House Historic Park 161, **161,** 162–163, 174
Charles Sumner School Museum and Archives 102–103

Cherry blossoms **64,** 64–65, **65,** 141
Chesapeake & Ohio Canal N.H.P. 17, **142,** 145, 146
Children, activities for 30–33
Chinatown **92,** 93, 138
Christ Church 161, **161,** 166, **170,** 170–171
Concerts, free 66–67, **67**
Cox's Row & around 144, 149, **149**
Crime 180
Cycling 26, 28–29, 65

D

Decatur House 20, 108, 111–112
Disabilities, travelers with 180
Discovery Theater 32
Downtown 86–105
  Chinatown **92,** 93, 138
  Ford's Theatre N.H.S. 9, 89, **89,** 91–93, 100
  Freedom Plaza 88, 90
  hotels 183–184
  International Spy Museum 87, 105, 154, 155
  map 88–89
  National Archives 9, 88, **88,** 90–91, **91**
  National Building Museum 32, **86,** 89, 95
  restaurants 95
  small museums 102–105, **103, 104**
  Smithsonian American Art Museum and National Portrait Gallery **9,** 25, 89, **89,** 93–94, 96-99
  theater scene 100–101
  Woolly Mammoth Theatre 89, 95
Dragon Boat Festival 140
Dumbarton House 145, 150–151, **151**
Dumbarton Oaks 144, **144,** 150, **152,** 152–153
Dupont Circle & beyond 126–141
  Adams Morgan 128, **128,** 134–135, **135,** 140, 184–186
  Anderson House 129, **130,** 131–132
  art galleries 131
  Dupont Circle 129–130
  Embassy Row **38,** 38–41, **39, 40**
  14th Street, N.W 27, **27,** 29, 129, 132–133
  hotels 184–186
  map 128–129
  multicultural Washington **138,** 138–139
  The Phillips Collection 129, **129,** 131, **136,** 136–137
  President Woodrow Wilson House 129, 132, **132**

restaurants 133
U Street, N.W **126,** 128, **128,** 133–134

E

Eastern Market 23, **23,** 24, 69, 70, **70,** 76–77, **77**
Eighth Street (Barracks Row) 69, 70, 77
Einstein Memorial 124
Ellipse 109, **116,** 116–117
Emancipation Memorial 124
Embassy of Brazil 39, 41
Embassy of Indonesia 39, 40, **40**
Embassy of South Africa 38, **38,** 41
Embassy Row **38,** 38–41, **39, 40**
Emergencies 180
Entertainment, free 66–67, **67**
Espionage **154,** 154–155, **155**
Ethnic restaurants 139, **139**

F

FDR Memorial 16, 49, **54,** 54–55
Festivals 65, 140–141, **141**
Fiesta DC 140
Fish Market 25, **25**
Floral Library 156
Folger Shakespeare Library 71, 76
Ford's Theatre N.H.S. 9, 89, **89,** 91–93, 100
Fort Ward Museum & Historic Site 175
14th Street, N.W. 27, **27,** 29, 129, 132–133
Franciscan Monastery 157, **157**
Franklin Delano Roosevelt Memorial 16, 49, **54,** 54–55
Frederick Douglass N.H.S. 35, 36
Free entertainment 66–67, **67**
Freedom Plaza 88, 90

G

Gadsby's Tavern Museum 161, 163–164, 174
Gardens 156–157, **157**
George Washington Masonic National Memorial 161, 166–167, **167**
Georgetown **42–43,** 142–157
  Chesapeake & Ohio Canal N.H.P. 17, **142,** 145, 146
  Cox's Row & around 144, 149, **149**
  D.C. in a day 14, 17
  D.C. in two days 18
  Dumbarton House 145, 150–151, **151**
  Dumbarton Oaks 144, **144,** 150, **152,** 152–153
  gardens 156–157, **157**

Georgetown University 144, **144**, 148
hotels 186–187
map 144–145
Oak Hill Chapel & Cemetery 145, 150
Old Stone House 145, 146
Prospect Street, N.W 144, 147–148
restaurants 150
row houses 148
shopping 26, 28
spies **154**, 154–155, **155**
Tudor Place Historic House & Garden 144, **144**, 149, 156
Washington Harbour 26, 28, 145, 147, **147**

H
Hamilton 16, 27, **27**, 29
Hawk 'n' Dove 84
Heurich House Museum 103–104
Hotels 181–187
Arlington, Virginia 187
Capitol Hill 181–182
downtown 183–184
Dupont Circle 184–186
Georgetown 186–187
Old Town Alexandria 187
White House & around 27, 29, 84, 85, 109, 117, 182–183

I
Independence Day 66
International Spy Museum 87, 105, 154, 155
Islamic Center of Washington 39, 40

J
J. Edgar Hoover FBI Building 88, 91
Jefferson Memorial **2–3**, 16, 49, 55

K
Kayaking 26, **26**, 28–29
Kennedy Center 14, **14**, 17, 18, 67
Kids, activities for 30–33
Korean War Veterans Memorial 48, **48**, 53
Kreeger Museum 104–105

L
Lafayette Square 16, 109, 110
Latino heritage 139, 140
Lee-Fendall House 161, 165, **165**
Library of Congress 17, 23, **23**, 24, 71, 72–73, **73**
Lincoln Memorial 16, 48, 52–53, **53**
Lincoln Theatre 35, **35**, 37
Living history museums 174–175, **175**

Lyceum, Alexandria's History Museum 160, 167–168

M
Maps
African-American heritage 34–35
Capitol Hill 70–71
D.C. for fun 26–27
D.C. in a day 14–15
D.C. in two days 18–19, 22–23
D.C. with kids 30–31
downtown 88–89
Dupont Circle & beyond 128–129
Embassy Row 38–39
Georgetown 144–145
National Mall 48–49
neighborhoods 44–45
Old Town Alexandria 160–161
White House & around 108–109
Martin Luther King, Jr. Memorial 16, 34, **34**, 36, 49, 54
Metro 179
The Monocle 84
Monuments & memorials 46–55
Adams Memorial 125
D.C. in a day 15, 16
Emancipation Memorial 124
FDR Memorial 16, 49, **54**, 54–55
Jefferson Memorial **2–3**, 16, 49, 55
Korean War Veterans Memorial 48, **48**, 53
Lincoln Memorial 16, 48, 52–53, **53**
Martin Luther King, Jr. Memorial 16, 34, **34**, 36, 49, 54
National World War II Memorial **5**, 16, 48, 51
Theodore Roosevelt Island National Memorial 25, 29, 125, **125**
Titanic Memorial 124
Vietnam Veterans Memorial 16, 48, **50**, 51–52
Washington Monument 9, 16, **46**, 48, 50
Mount Vernon 169, 174–175, **175**
Mr. Henry's 37

N
National Air & Space Museum 15, **15**, 16, 19, 49, 57, **60**, 60–63, **63**
National Archives 9, 88, **88**, 90–91, **91**
National Building Museum 32, **86**, 89, 95
National Cathedral 30, **30**, 32, 38, 41
National Cherry Blossom Festival 141
National Christmas Tree 116, **116**
National Gallery of Art 19, **19**, 21, 49, 55, 56–57, 66
National Geographic Society 108,

108, 112
National Harbor, Maryland 31, 33
National Law Enforcement Memorial and Museum 89, 95
National Mall 46–67
Castle 20, 51
cherry blossoms **64**, 64–65, **65**, 141
D.C. in two days 19
definition 52
Franklin Delano Roosevelt Memorial 16, 49, **54**, 54–55
free entertainment 66–67, **67**
Korean War Veterans Memorial 48, **48**, 53
Lincoln Memorial 16, 48, 52–53, **53**
map 48–49
Martin Luther King, Jr. Memorial 16, 34, **34**, 36, 49, 54
National Air & Space Museum 15, **15**, 16, 19, 49, 57, **60**, 60–63, **63**
National Gallery of Art 19, **19**, 21, 49, 55, 56–57, 66
National Museum of American History 19, 20, 55, **58**, 58–59
National Museum of Natural History 20, 32, 49, **49**, 56, **57**
National World War II Memorial **5**, 16, 48, 51
restaurants 55
Thomas Jefferson Memorial **2–3**, 16, 49, 55
Vietnam Veterans Memorial 16, 48, **50**, 51–52
Washington Monument 9, 16, **46**, 48, 50
National Museum of African American History and Culture 20, 34, 36, **36**
National Museum of American History 19, 20, 55, **58**, 58–59
National Museum of Natural History 20, 32, 49, **49**, 56, **57**
National Museum of the American Indian 21, **21**, 55
National Museum of Women in the Arts 102, **103**
National Portrait Gallery **5**, **9**, 89, 93–94, **94**, 96–99
National Postal Museum 102
National Theater 100, **100**
National World War II Memorial **5**, 16, 48, 51
National Zoological Park 30, **30**, 32

O
Oak Hill Chapel & Cemetery 145, 150
Observatory Circle 38, 41
Octagon House 16, 20, 109, 114
Old Ebbitt Grill 22, 25, 85, **85**

Old Stone House 145, 146
Old Town Alexandria 158–175
  Alexandria Visitor Center at Ramsay House 161, 162
  Carlyle House Historic Park 161, **161**, 162–163, 174
  Christ Church 161, **161**, 166, **170**, 170–171
  churches 171
  colonial Alexandria **172**, 172–173, **173**
  Gadsby's Tavern Museum 161, 163–164, 174
  George Washington Masonic National Memorial 161, 166–167, **167**
  hotels 187
  Lee-Fendall House 161, 165, **165**
  living history 174–175, **175**
  Lyceum, Alexandria's History Museum 160, 167–168
  map 160–161
  restaurants 166
  Scottish Christmas Walk Weekend 141
  Stabler-Leadbeater Apothecary Museum 160, **160**, **168**, 168–169, 174
  Torpedo Factory Art Center 160, **160**, 169
Organization of American States 109, 114–115, **115**

P
Paddleboating 31, 33, **33**, 64–65
Penn Quarter **4**, 22, 25
The Phillips Collection 129, **129**, 131, **136**, 136–137
Potomac River kayaking and biking 26, **26**, 28–29
POV bar **5**, 25, 84
President Lincoln's Cottage 105
President Woodrow Wilson House 129, 132, **132**
Presidential Washington **122**, 122–123, **123**
Prospect Street, N.W 144, 147–148

R
Renwick Gallery 108, 112–113, **113**
Restaurants
  bars **5**, 25, 84–85, **85**
  Capitol Hill 37, 75
  downtown 95
  Dupont Circle & beyond 133
  Georgetown 150
  international cuisine 139, **139**
  National Mall 55

Old Ebbitt Grill 22, 25, 85, **85**
  Old Town Alexandria 166
  Penn Quarter 25
  White House & around 111
River Farm 157
Rock Creek Park 25
Round Robin Bar 85

S
Scottish Christmas Walk Weekend 141
Security measures 8–9, 178
Sheridan Circle 39, 40
Smithsonian American Art Museum **9**, 25, 89, **89**, 93–94, 96–99
Smithsonian Castle 20, 51
Smithsonian Folklife Festival 141, **141**
Smithsonian Institution
  events 21, 141, **141**
  overview 51
Southwest Waterfront 25, **25**
Spies **154**, 154–155, **155**
Spite House 164
St. John's Episcopal Church 108, **108**, 110
St. Patrick's Day Parade 140
Stabler-Leadbeater Apothecary Museum 160, **160**, **168**, 168–169, 174
Statues, secret 124–125, **125**
Supreme Court 17, 23, 24, 71, **74**, 74–75

T
Theater scene **100**, 100–101, **101**
Theodore Roosevelt Island National Memorial 25, 29, 125, **125**
Thomas Jefferson Memorial **2–3**, 16, 49, 55
Tidal Basin 31, 33, **33**, **64**, 64–65, **65**, 141
Titanic Memorial 124
Torpedo Factory Art Center 160, **160**, 169
Transportation 179–180
Tudor Place Historic House & Garden 144, **144**, 149, 156

U
U Street, N.W **126**, 128, **128**, 133–134
Udvar-Hazy Center 62
Union Station 70, **70**, 72
U.S. Botanic Garden 24, 156
U.S. Capitol
  design 69, **83**
  Emancipation Hall 17, 24, 79
  free concerts 66, **67**
  in-depth **78**, 78–81, **81**

on map 23, 71
  National Statuary Hall **68**, 80–81
  Visitor Center 17, 24, 79
  visitor information 17, 24, 72
U.S. National Arboretum 25, 65
U.S. Supreme Court 17, 23, 24, 71, **74**, 74–75

V
Vietnam Veterans Memorial 16, 48, **50**, 51–52
Visitor information 178

W
W Washington D.C. hotel 27, **27**, 29, 84, 183
Washington Harbour 26, 28, 145, 147, **147**
Washington Monument 9, 16, **46**, 48, 50
Washington National Cathedral 30, **30**, 32, 38, 41
Washington Nationals baseball team 123
White House & around 106–125
  Art Museum of the Americas & Organization of American States 109, 114–115, **115**
  D.C. in a day 15, **15**, 16
  D.C. in two days 19, 20
  Decatur House 20, 108, 111–112
  Ellipse 109, **116**, 116–117
  hotels 27, **27**, 29, 84, 85, 109, 117, 182–183
  Lafayette Square 16, 109, 110
  map 108–109
  National Christmas Tree 116, **116**
  National Geographic Society 108, **108**, 112
  Octagon House 16, 20, 109, 114
  presidential Washington **122**, 122–123, **123**
  Renwick Gallery 108, 112–113, **113**
  restaurants 111
  secret statues 124–125, **125**
  St. John's Episcopal Church 108, **108**, 110
  White House **6**, **106**, 109, **109**, **110**, **118**, 118–121, **121**
  Willard InterContinental 85, 109, 117
Willard InterContinental 85, 109, 117, 183
Woolly Mammoth Theatre 89, 95
World War II Memorial **5**, 16, 48, 51

Y
The Yards Park 67, 72

INDEX

CREDITS

Walking Washington

Barbara Noe Kennedy

Since 1888, the National Geographic Society has funded more than 14,000 research, exploration, and preservation projects around the world. National Geographic Partners distributes a portion of the funds it receives from your purchase to National Geographic Society to support programs including the conservation of animals and their habitats.

National Geographic Partners, LLC
1145 17th Street NW
Washington, DC 20036-4688 USA

Get closer to National Geographic explorers and photographers, and connect with our global community. Join us today at nationalgeographic.org/joinus

For rights or permissions inquiries, please contact National Geographic Books Subsidiary Rights: bookrights@natgeo.com

Copyright © 2017, 2021 National Geographic Partners, LLC. All rights reserved. Reproduction of the whole or any part of the contents without written permission from the publisher is prohibited.

NATIONAL GEOGRAPHIC and Yellow Border Design are trademarks of the National Geographic Society, used under license.

Edition edited by White Star s.r.l.
Licensee of National Geographic Partners, LLC.
Update by Christopher P. Baker

The information in this book has been carefully checked and to the best of our knowledge is accurate. However, details are subject to change, and the publisher cannot be responsible for such changes, or for errors or omissions. Assessments of sites, hotels, and restaurants are based on the author's subjective opinions, which do not necessarily reflect the publisher's opinion.

ISBN: 978-88-544-1712-0

Printed in China
23/TL/2

MIX
Paper from
responsible sources
FSC® C178000

CREDITS

Author

Barbara Noe Kennedy

All photographs by Lisa A. Walker unless otherwise indicated below:

Picture Credits
T = top, b = bottom,
l = left, r = right

4 Oomka/Shutterstock. **19r** OPIS Zagreb/Shutterstock. **21** Cvandyke/Shutterstock. com. **22** mervas/Shutterstock. **25** Sean Pavone/Shutterstock. **26** Orhan Cam/ Shutterstock. **27b** Viktor1/ Shutterstock. **28** Bill O'Leary/ The *Washington Post* via Getty Images. **30l** MrNikolay/Shutterstock. **36** Ricky Carioti/ The *Washington Post* via Getty Images. **49** NaughtyNut/ Shutterstock. **58** Marvin Joseph/The *Washington Post* via Getty Images. **63** NYC Russ/Shutterstock. **67** U.S. Navy photo by Chief Musician Brian P. Bowman/ Released. **78** f11photo/Shutterstock. **82** Harris & Ewing Collection/Library of Congress Prints and Photographs Division. **83** Universal History Archive/UIG via Getty

Images. **89t** Bumble Dee/ Shutterstock. **89b** Olivier Douliery/Getty Images. **91** The *Washington Post*/Getty Images. **100** Evgenia Parajanian/Shutterstock. **101** Nicole Glass Photography/ Shutterstock. **104** Kelly/ Mooney Photography/Getty Images. **115** Rob Crandall/ Shutterstock. **116** Paul Franklin/Alamy Stock Photo. **122** *Chicago Tribune*/Getty Images. **123** Joseph Sohm/Shutterstock. **126** Truba7113/Shutterstock. **128b** ton koene/ Alamy Stock Photo. **130** The *Washington Post*/Getty Images. **132** Everett Collection/Shutterstock. **141** Roberto Galan/Shutterstock. **142** Danita Delimont/Alamy Stock Photo. **152** Charles Kogod/Getty Images. **154** Don Emmert/Getty Images. **155** Erik Cox Photography/ Shutterstock. **157** Cvandyke/ Shutterstock.com. **160t** Joseph Gidjunis, JPG Photography. **165** Everett Historical/ Shutterstock. **167** MISHELLA/Shutterstock. **173** Jon Bilous/Shutterstock.

Created by Mary Norris Creative Services

Mary Luders Norris, *Editorial Director*

Marty Ittner, *Designer*

Maggie Smith, *Cartographer*